Bill Mantovani

Sage 50 Payroll 2016

For users of Sage 50 Payroll 2016, Sage 50 Payroll Professional 2016 and Sage One Payroll

In easy steps is an imprint of In Easy Steps Limited
16 Hamilton Terrace · Holly Walk · Leamington Spa
Warwickshire · United Kingdom · CV32 4LY
www.ineasysteps.com

Notice of Liability
Every effort has been made to ensure that this book contains accurate
and current information. However, In Easy Steps Limited and the
author shall not be liable for any loss or damage suffered by readers
as a result of any information contained herein.

Trademarks
Sage 50® is a registered trademark of The Sage Group plc.
All other trademarks are acknowledged as belonging to their
respective companies.

In Easy Steps Limited supports The Forest Stewardship Council (FSC),
the leading international forest certification organisation. All our titles
that are printed on Greenpeace approved FSC certified paper carry the
FSC logo.

MIX
Paper from
responsible sources
FSC® C020837

Printed and bound in the United Kingdom

ISBN 978-1-84078-717-7

Contents

9 Statutory Sick Pay 113

10 Statutory Maternity Pay 123

11 Company Pension Scheme 133

12 Deductions, Loans and Attachments 141

1 Getting Started

This chapter takes you through the stages of preparing Sage 50 Payroll for use. It explains initial procedures for setting up options and defaults before you start entering data.

Certain tasks need completing to set up payroll and pay your employees for the first time, such as registering as an employer and for reporting payroll online with HMRC and telling them about your employees. You normally have to operate PAYE as part of your payroll.

To avoid making mistakes on your company payroll, you can always practice on the demonstration data first. See page 22.

Whilst Sage 50 Payroll is a flexible, user friendly program, it is still very important to ensure you enter payroll information carefully and accurately.

Introduction

For many businesses, manual payroll was a very laborious task but with the introduction of Real Time Information (RTI) in recent HMRC legislation, the mandatory online submission of payroll information now makes reporting much quicker. This is covered in Chapters 13 and 15. However, as there are a minor number of exceptions where paper submission is still allowed, the manual production of various reports has been covered where applicable.

This book explains and describes in easy to follow stages how to computerise your payroll requirements using the Sage 50 Payroll package. It is full of handy hints and advice about how to enter, maintain and process your information quickly and easily and thus avoid making costly mistakes. It takes you through, in a step-by-step guide, the various stages involved in running a payroll system and covers important payroll and HMRC legislation changes.

Sage produce several versions of Sage 50 Payroll depending on number of employees, users and companies. Sage Instant Payroll is for small businesses with a maximum of five employees. Most of this book is relevant to all versions, though some features are specific to only certain versions.

Preparing to use Sage 50 Payroll

Before you can do any payroll processing, a certain amount of preparation is required. Employee, Company and Government legislation information should be checked so that complex tasks such as Tax Calculations, NI, SSP/SMP and holiday entitlements can be processed quickly and easily without error. This book guides you through all of this preparation in easy to follow steps.

Employee and Company records store very detailed information. Because of the confidential nature of payroll, this book shows you how to set up passwords and different levels of security to protect this information from unauthorised access.

Many statutory forms are produced during payroll processing. You will be advised of the various forms and reports required at different stages (handy for a business that may be exempt online submission), and of the importance of regularly backing up your payroll data.

You are also shown how to ensure you have the latest version of the program and up-to-date Government legislation by using the automated update facility.

Overview

The concepts used by Sage Payroll are very easy to grasp and are similar to the once manual system. It basically records information using three sets of 'cards' – the Employee Record card, the Payment card and a single Legislation card for the entire payroll.

For every employee there is an Employee Record card to store information such as Name, National Insurance Number, Tax Code and Payment Details etc. This information is grouped into a number of sections, accessed by clicking on the corresponding tab.

The following is an example of an Employee Record and shows Employment details:

Use the Quick Employee option from the Employee Tasks list to speed up entering a new employee's details (see page 58).

| Personal | Employment | Pensions | Absence | Cars/Fuel | Banking | Analysis | History | Terms | Documents |

Job Title

Tax Code * 749L   Week 1/Month 1 Basis ☐
NI Category * A   Manual NI Entry ☐
N.I. Number * JE 875764 C
Starter Form

Start Date * 01/02/2006   Welfare To Work ☐
Leave Date / /   FPS Starter ☐
Status OK   Non-UK Worker ☐
RTI Payroll ID c7773b5f43114c8188167829fae5715e

Operate net of foreign tax credit relief ☑

Works Number 2
Director Status Non-Director
Payment Method BACS
Payment Frequency Weekly
Employment Type

Student Loan Start 28/04/2010
Student Loan Type Plan Type 1
Student Loan End / /
Student Loan Priority 0
Protected Earnings 0.00

[Pay Elements] [Salary] [YTD Values] [Leaver] [Apprentice]

For every employee, there is also an Employee Payment card, such as the one below, for recording Basic Pay, Overtime Rates and Bonuses, together with any regular Deductions, Attachments, Loans and Salary Sacrifice, etc.

Make sure you are always up-to-date with the latest Government legislation information relating to payroll.

| Payments | Deductions | Loans | Attachment of Earnings Orders | Salary Sacrifice |

Payment Name	Tax	NI	Hours/No.	Multiplier	Amt/Perc	Rate	Base Payment	In Use
Salary	Pre	Pre	35.0000	N/A	N/A	5.6000	N/A	Yes
Bonus	Pre	Pre	1.0000	N/A	N/A	100.0000	N/A	Yes
Overtime	Pre	Pre	1.0000	N/A	N/A	0.0000	N/A	Yes

Beware

When in doubt, check! Some employees will not be happy if you make a mistake that then needs correcting in the next pay period.

Hot tip

For instant help in any Sage window, simply press the F1 key at any time to bring up the detailed Help facility.

Hot tip

You can link Sage Payroll to Sage 50 accounting software and make automated postings to update your Profit and Loss and Balance Sheet with payroll journals.

...cont'd

Location of Payroll Data

The installation procedure copies all the necessary files onto your PC for you, though it is sometimes handy to know how Sage 50 Payroll is stored on your computer.

Typically, the Payroll program will be stored on drive C:, in the PROGRAM FILES\SAGE PAYROLL folder, whilst data is stored in the PROGRAMDATA\SAGE\PAYROLL folder. This folder is then further sub-divided as follows:

PAYROLL\COMPANY.001	contains the PAYDATA and PICTURES folders (see the Note below).
PAYROLL\COMPANY.001\PAYDATA	holds all of the Employee Records, payments and parameter details.
PAYROLL\COMPANY.001\PICTURES	contains the bitmap files of employee photos to go with the respective records, where used.
PAYROLL\REPORTS	holds the report files available to you within the Payroll program.
PAYROLL\TEMPLATE	holds the Stationery layout templates such as Payslips, Giros, Cheques.

Multi-company versions will have COMPANY.001, COMPANY.002, etc.

Note: the above are the default file locations for recent versions of Sage 50 Payroll. You can, however, choose to specify different locations during the initial program installation.

Working through Sage 50 Payroll in easy steps

This book explains how to perform the main tasks required for keeping a computerised payroll system. The following chapters show you how to:

- Check and amend Government legislation settings

- Record comprehensive Employee and Company details

- Provide Payroll Security

- Create a nominal link to Sage 50 Accounts

- Pay your Employees weekly, fortnightly or monthly

- Deal with Statutory Sick Pay, Statutory Maternity Pay, SAP, SPP and SPP(A)

- Record and maintain your Company Pension Schemes

- Set up and process Deductions and Attachments

- Process Payroll runs and print Statutory Forms

- Run your Year End Routine

- Carry out File Maintenance

Preparing to start checklist

The secret to running an accurate payroll system is to have all relevant information to hand at all times. Therefore, make sure you have, or have done the following before using your Payroll program for the first time:

- Collated all your Employee Record information

- Checked your government parameters are recorded correctly

- Have company details and pay elements to hand

- Planned, then checked, your nominal link settings

- Decided how you will implement payroll security

- Set up a backup strategy or facility

Remember that you can familiarise yourself with Payroll's features and practice with the demonstration company provided with the program until you are ready to start entering your own data for real.

Why not let the Payroll Year End Wizard guide you quickly through the Year End procedure.

11

Remember to maintain your internet connection if you wish to make use of the news feeds, automatic updates, e-submissions and other online facilities available in Payroll.

Key Functions

The following shortcut features are available to help you whilst working with your Sage 50 Payroll program. Make full use of them to save time.

Function keys and Keystrokes are provided for frequently used actions. Practice using them regularly and you will find your Payroll program easier to use.

Function keys

F1   Opens the online help system.

F2   Displays your computer's calculator.

F3   Opens the Sage Help Map that guides you through the payroll process.

F4   Displays the calendar, calculator or Finder search if the selected box has any of these special buttons attached.

F8   Clears the content of a field.

F12   Minimises the Sage Payroll program.

Function Keys F5, F6, F7, F9, F10 and F11 can be user-defined by selecting View, then Options and clicking on the Function Keys tab from the Sage Payroll Desktop.

To user-define your Function Keys, click Options from the Desktop window, select the Function Keys tab and use the Finder button to enter an action of your choice.

Keystrokes

Esc	Exits the current screen without saving.
Tab	Accepts an entry and moves to the next field or entry box.
Shift + Tab	Moves back to the previous field or box.
End	Moves the cursor to the last character of the last word in the field.
Home	Moves the cursor to the start of the field.
Ctrl + Right Arrow	Moves to the first character of the next word in the field.
Ctrl + Left Arrow	Moves the cursor to the first character of the previous word in the field.
Ctrl + N (or n)	Advances to the next selected record.
Ctrl + P (or p)	Moves back to the previous record.

A quick method of accessing an option from the menu bar is to hold down the Alt key and press the underlined letter of the function required (i.e., Alt + T (or t) pulls down the Tasks menu).

The Payroll Desktop

The Payroll Desktop features a menu bar, navigation groups, links and tasks on the left side, and a switchable split screen with tree view on the left and list view on the right.

The main program options are quickly accessed using the stacked groups by clicking on the Payroll, Employee, Company, Desktop, etc. buttons. Many of these options are also available from Tasks on the menu bar. The toolbar above the list view area provides additional list selection and reporting functions.

Payroll Desktop

1 Use the Tasks option on the toolbar for functions not shown in the navigation groups

2 Main payroll functions can be quickly selected in this area

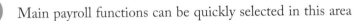

3 The list area shows a list of Employee Records

4 The Outline button on the toolbar is used to hide the tree view when not required

5 Double-click an employee in the list view to quickly open the Employee Record window

Hot tip

Use the Health Check button from the toolbar to quickly see if any errors have occurred.

Don't forget

Remember that you can rearrange the fields in the list view to suit your requirements. Simply drag a field to a new position with the left button of your mouse.

Hot tip

Use the Criteria button from the toolbar to quickly filter employee information.

Hot tip

To sort by a particular field just click on the field name at the top of the column.

Hot tip

Clicking on the Outline button in the toolbar removes the tree view and maximises the list view, allowing you to see more record columns.

Don't forget

To restore the tree view just click on the Outline button again.

...cont'd

Sorting your information to meet requirements

When required, you can easily sort your payroll information into a different order. For example, to sort your employees by surname order do the following:

 Click once here to sort into ascending order (A-Z)

 To revert the sort to its original order simply click again

Reorganising your columns

To reorganise the employee column list, do the following:

 Using the left mouse button, simply drag the chosen column to a new required position

Setting up Desktop Options

You can change the appearance of the Desktop to suit your preferences. The following options are available:

Toolbars

1 From the menu bar click View, then Options and select the Environment tab

2 Tick how you want text labels shown on the toolbar

3 Change the list style to the older style if you prefer

4 Select the initial Desktop view here

5 Make Preview the Report default to save printer paper

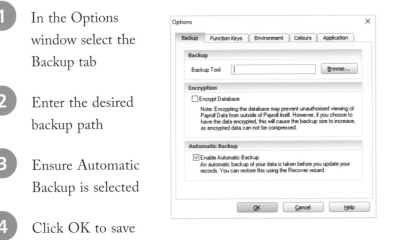

Backup
To set the backup drive location:

1 In the Options window select the Backup tab

2 Enter the desired backup path

3 Ensure Automatic Backup is selected

4 Click OK to save selection and close

Quickly define your own shortcut keys by selecting the Function Keys tab. Here you can user define six additional keys. See page 16.

Use the Browse... button to help you find a path for your Payroll backups.

To exit without saving your changes, just click on the Cancel button.

Press F12 at any time to minimise your screen, instantly hiding confidential information from view.

...cont'd

Function Keys

You can also set up some of the keyboard Function keys to open application programs for you. To set up a Function key:

1 From the menu bar click View, then Options and select the Function Keys tab

2 Decide which Function key you wish to define

3 Use the Finder button to browse for an application

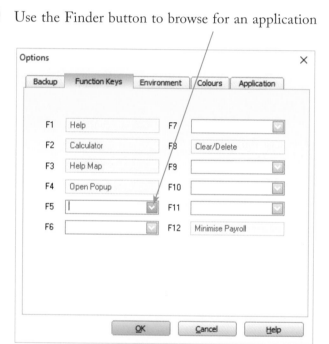

Don't forget

Key functions shown in grey in the Function Key window, such as F1, F2, F8 etc., are pre-programmed by Sage and cannot be altered.

4 Select the program and click Open

5 Click OK to save, or Cancel to abort

...cont'd

Colours

To set up your colour defaults, do the following:

1 From the menu bar click View, then Options

2 Click the Colours tab

3 To use colours, ensure Ignore colours is not ticked

4 Use this box to change text colours for each option

Hot tip

If you do not want to show colours, simply tick the Ignore colours box.

Options   ✕

| Backup | Function Keys | Environment | Colours | Application |

☐ Ignore colours

Alternate Employee Lines

Employee Highlight

Note that if your computer displays less than 16-bit colour, only the solid colours shown here will match the actual colours used by the program.

Revert to Defaults

OK   Cancel   Help

5 Select the colour required

6 Click OK

7 Use the other button to change the highlight colour for each option

8 Repeat Steps 5 & 6, then click OK to close the Options window

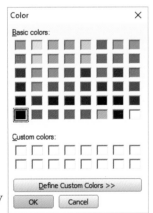

Color   ✕

Basic colors:

Custom colors:

Define Custom Colors >>

OK   Cancel

Don't forget

You can also define your own colours by clicking the Define Custom Colors >> button in the Color window.

17

Using Criteria

This feature is very useful for quickly supplying you with categorised levels of employee information, e.g. a list of weekly paid staff together with their department. You can also use the Criteria option for excluding unnecessary records from your processing list, such as Leavers, staff On Holiday and those On Hold.

The following example shows you how to list only employees who are paid weekly in cash:

1 Click the Criteria button on the toolbar

2 In the Filter list select the By Payment Period filter

3 Then filter By Payment Method

4 Set the last filter to None

5 Ensure only Weekly and Cash is selected

6 Tick to Exclude Employees as required

Criteria dialog:

Filter Employee List — By Payment Period
then Filter — By Payment Method
then Filter — None

Include these Pay Frequencies:
- Fortnightly ☐ Monthly ☐
- Four Weekly ☐ Weekly ☑

Include these Pay Methods:
- BACS ☐ Cheque ☐
- Cash ☑ Credit Transfer ☐
- Direct BACS ☐ Sage Payments ☐

Exclude Employees who are:
- On Hold ☑ On Holiday ☐
- Current Year Leavers ☑ Historical Leavers ☑

OK Cancel

7 Click OK to accept the settings and close the window

8 To see the filter in action, in the tree view double-click on All Employees to invoke your selection and bring up the Weekly folder only

9 Finally, double-click on Weekly, then Cash. The list view now shows only those employees paid weekly in cash

Hot tip

You can also run the Criteria function by simply clicking on the Criteria icon in the Desktop Tasks area.

Beware

It is always advisable to reset the Criteria filters once you have finished to avoid confusion later. It is not uncommon for a user to forget they have set a filter and later think they have somehow deleted employees!

Don't forget

Remember that you will not see Employee Lists that match your selected criteria until you step down the appropriate levels in the tree view.

Government Legislation

Government legislation can change from time to time, such as when there's a Chancellor's Budget. Sage Payroll comes with settings for legislation relating to the current tax year. If legislation changes for a new tax year then this will be included in updates or the latest software, which can be downloaded from the Sage website.

However, before you start entering employee and company details it is advisable to familiarise yourself with your current payroll legislation settings, as follows:

1 Click Company in the navigation group

2 Click Legislation... in the Tasks pane

3 From the PAYE tab check the Bandwidths and Rates. Details can be changed should it become necessary

These settings should not need changing unless there is a change to Government legislation.

You can also use the Reports option from the toolbar to print out and check current legislation settings and information.

Legislation Settings - 2016/2017

Tabs: PAYE | NI Bands & Rates | SSP | SMP/SAP/SPP/ShPP | Car Details | Student | AEO Rates | Minimum Wage | Childcare | Automatic Enrolment

Tax bandwidths and rates effective from 06/04/2016 — Add Date | Edit Date | Delete Date

Bandwidth	From	To	Rest of UK Rate (%)	Scottish Rate (%)	Basic Rate Band
32000.00	0.01	32000.00	20.00	20.00	Yes
118000.00	32000.01	150000.00	40.00	40.00	No
excess	150000.01	excess	45.00	45.00	No

Number of Tax Bands: 3
Emergency Tax Code: 1100L
Regulatory Deduction Limit %: 50

☑ Check for online legislation updates
☑ Prompt before performing check

The Legislation Settings shown are for the 2016/2017 Tax Year   OK   Cancel

4 When finished, click OK to save and close or Cancel to discard any changes and close the Legislation Settings window

Regularly refer to the HMRC website, **www. hmrc.gov.uk** for the most up to date legislation information.

Beware

It is very important to remember that you should not edit these bandwidths or rates unless government legislation changes, or unless you are advised to do so by Sage.

Hot tip

If you make a mistake and accidentally alter a setting, simply click on the Cancel button.

Don't forget

Statutory Payments are recorded via the Absence tab of the individual Employee Records.

...cont'd

To check SSP and SMP/SAP/SPP legislation settings

It is also important to be very familiar with Statutory Sick Pay, Statutory Maternity Pay, Statutory Adoption Pay, and Statutory Paternity Pay legislation. To check the settings for the current payroll year, do the following:

 Click Legislation... in the Company Tasks pane

2 Click on the SSP tab and note the settings

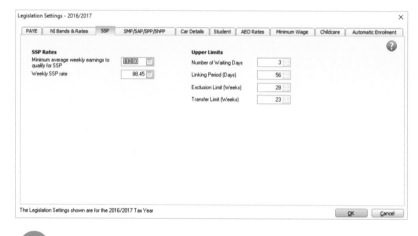

3 Next, check the settings on the SMP/SAP/SPP/ShPP tab

 When finished, click OK to close the Legislation Settings window or Cancel to discard any changes

To check Car Details and Car Bands

Another area that can change in annual budgets is the legislation for the use of company cars. Check and familiarise yourself with these rates as follows:

 1 Click Legislation... in the Company Tasks pane

2 Check settings in the Car Details tab, then click the Rates button to view CO2 Emissions details

Legislation was introduced in a past budget regarding the liability for National Insurance contributions (NIC) on the value of company cars and the fuel they use. Employers are liable for NIC on the value of company cars and fuel provided by them. Therefore, accurate records need to be kept of business mileage for each company car.

CO2 Emissions

Emission Scale Charge

CO2/g	Petrol %	Diesel % (incl. Euro IV reg'd on or after 01/01/06)	Diesel % (Euro IV reg'd on or before 31/12/05)
0	5.00	3.00	3.00
1	5.00	3.00	3.00
51	9.00	3.00	3.00
76	13.00	3.00	3.00
95	14.00	3.00	3.00
100	15.00	3.00	3.00
105	16.00	3.00	3.00
110	17.00	3.00	3.00
115	18.00	3.00	3.00
120	19.00	3.00	3.00
125	20.00	3.00	3.00
130	21.00	3.00	3.00
135	22.00	3.00	3.00
140	23.00	3.00	3.00
145	24.00	3.00	3.00
150	25.00	3.00	3.00
155	26.00	3.00	3.00
160	27.00	3.00	3.00
165	28.00	3.00	3.00
170	29.00	3.00	3.00
175	30.00	3.00	3.00
180	31.00	3.00	3.00
185	32.00	3.00	3.00
190	33.00	3.00	3.00

No Approved CO2 Emissions

CC From	CC To	Petrol %	Diesel %
1	1400	15.00	18.00
1401	2000	25.00	28.00
2001	Excess	37.00	37.00

Cars Registered Before 01/01/1998

CC From	CC To	Charge %
1	1400	15.00
1401	2000	25.00
2001	Excess	37.00

Fuel Reductions

Fuel Type	% Reduction
Electricity Only	0.00
Hybrid Electric	0.00
Bi-Fuel	0.00
Conversion	0.00
E85 (Bio-Ethanol)	0.00

Legislation Settings - 2016/2017

Tabs: PAYE | NI Bands & Rates | ... | Automatic Enrolment

Car Values
Maximum Car List Price
Maximum Capital Contribution
Minimum Accessory Value

New Cars
New cars - Up to (years)
Date cars aged against

Company car fuel rate
HMRC Set Figure

Rates

The Legislation Settings shown are for...

Cancel

Close

Repayment of student loans

1 Click on the Student tab to view the income thresholds

Legislation Settings - 2016/2017

Tabs: PAYE | NI Bands & Rates | SSP | SMP/SAP/SPP/ShPP | Car Details | Student | AEO Rates | Minimum Wage | Childcare | Automatic Enrolment

Student Loans Rates

Type	Weekly Threshold	Monthly Threshold	Annual Threshold	Rate
Plan Type 1	336.44	1457.91	17495.00	9.00
Plan Type 2	403.84	1750.00	21000.00	9.00

The Legislation Settings shown are for the 2016/2017 Tax Year

OK   Cancel

2 When done, click OK to close

Current legislation requires that the collection of any student loan repayments be made through the payroll system.

Demonstration Data

To help you become familiar with Payroll and all of its features without using your own company data, you are provided with demonstration data to practice on. To open the demonstration company, simply do the following:

1 From the File menu choose Open Company...

2 Select Demonstration Data from the list

3 Click OK to bring up the Log On screen

4 Note the processing date and tax period

5 Click OK to open the demonstration data

6 When finished, to return to your own company data, simply repeat the above steps

22

2 Payroll Security

Learn how to set up your Payroll security so that only authorised users can access data. This includes creating users, giving access rights and adding a password.

User Names and Access Rights

Sage Payroll provides you with the facility to restrict access to the system to authorised users only. After installation, initial access to the program is available via the user name MANAGER. Unless you give permission to another user, it is recommended that only the MANAGER should set up access rights or create users.

Using the Security options from the Tasks menu, the MANAGER can create a number of users and passwords. Users can then be restricted from various areas of the Payroll program.

Setting a MANAGER password

When you first install Sage Payroll, no password is allocated to the user name MANAGER, so the first thing you should do is to set one up otherwise the payroll system is left open to unauthorised access. To do this:

You must log on as MANAGER the first time you use Sage Payroll, though a password will not be required.

 Click on Tasks on the menu bar

 Select Security, then click on Change Personal Password...

3 Enter your Password in the New Password box

When you use Sage Payroll for the first time, remember to secure your data by setting up a password for MANAGER.

4 Enter your password again in the Confirm New Password box

5 Click OK to save your password and close, or Cancel to abandon

Access

Having logged onto the Payroll system as MANAGER, you can now set up new users. Each user can then be allocated their own password and different areas and levels of access, as appropriate. The list below highlights the different payroll access areas offered.

Access	Company Areas
Payroll:	Reset Payments, Timesheet Entry Enter Payments, Update and Nominal Link
Company:	Company Details (Edit, New & Delete) Pension Schemes, Holidays Pay Elements and Nominal Settings Legislation, Salary Review Historical Data (not available to Sage Instant Payroll users)
Employee:	Employee Record, Employee Wizard Quick Employee, Personnel Record YTD Values, P45/P46 Information Leaver and Delete Employee
Reports:	Pre/Post-update Reports Main and Custom Reports
e-Submissions:	Settings, Log, IR Secure Mailbox Collector of Taxes
Utilities:	Global Changes (Tax Codes, NI Categories, Pay Elements, Pensions) Upgrade Program, Rollback Data Backup and Restore Import/Export Data, Reminders Payroll Year End and e-Banking
Access Rights:	Access Rights Change Program Password
Microsoft Integration:	Send Messages, Export to MS Excel Send to MS Outlook, MS Outlook Tasks, MS Word Mail Merge

Note: Not all of the above areas are available in different versions of the Sage Payroll program.

Once you have set up a password for MANAGER, you must be very careful never to lose it.

Before processing your first payroll, take some time to work out the security levels you need. You can then set these up as shown in the following pages.

For security reasons and to avoid problems later, it is always advisable to structure your payroll access rights so that each authorised user can only access their own particular area of work.

Setting up a User

Start the Sage Payroll program and log in as MANAGER. You are now in a position to create a new user and set up their password. To do this, do the following:

A Logon Name can be up to 30 characters, whilst a Password can be up to 10 characters and is not case sensitive.

1 Click on Tasks on the menu bar

2 Select Security, then click on Access Rights...

3 The Access Rights Window shows existing users and their access rights

Leaving the Password box blank means the user will not need a password to access Sage Payroll. It also means anyone else who knows the user name can also access Payroll!

4 Click Add

5 Enter Logon Name for the new user

6 Enter the user Password

7 Click OK to accept

To set up access rights immediately after you add a user, after doing Step 8 continue from Step 3 on Page 27.

8 Click Save to save changes and close the Access Rights window

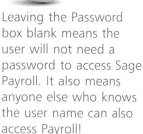

26

Allocating Access Rights

Having decided which areas of the program you want each of your users to have access to, you are now ready to allocate those access rights. Note that this facility is not available to Sage Instant Payroll users.

1 Click on Tasks on the menu bar

2 Select Security, then click on Access Rights...

3 The Access Rights Window shows existing users and their access rights

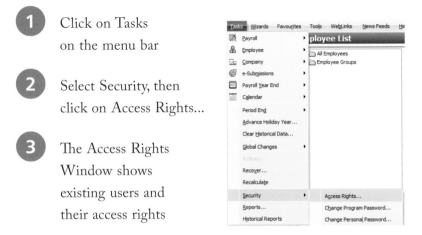

Simply click on the Select All button to allocate access to all areas to a user. Use the Clear button to deselect all access settings.

4 Click on the user you wish to set access rights for

5 Tick to allow or untick to refuse access to an area, here

Where user access to an area is prohibited, the icon will appear in grey.

6 Set the other access levels as required, then click Save

27

Editing User Names

Sage Payroll allows you to edit user names, access rights and passwords. To do this however, the task must be carried out by the manager or another user with access to the Access Rights area.

To edit a user's Access Rights, do the following:

 From the menu bar, click Tasks, then Security and Access Rights... to bring up the Access Rights window

 Select the user whose access details need amending

 Edit the user's access rights here by ticking to allow or removing the tick to refuse user access to a particular area

Hot tip

When a user leaves and a new one takes over the same tasks, save time and just edit the previous user name and password to the new details.

Access Rights — □ ✕

Users
MANAGER
Bill

[Add] [Edit] [Delete]

Employee Record Access

Weekly	☑	Fortnightly	☑
Four Weekly	☑	Monthly	☑
Access Level	0	Include lower levels	☑

Suppress Non-Essential Messaging

Employee Record	☐	Processing	☐
Other	☐	Automatic Enrolment	☐

Allow Access To These Areas:
- ☑ Personnel Record
  - ☑ Appraisal
  - ☐ Disciplinary
  - ☑ Job History
- ☑ YTD Values
- ☑ P45/P46 Information
- ☑ Leaver
- ☐ Delete Employee
- ☐ Statement of Employment
- ☑ Company
  - ☐ Settings
    - ☐ Details
    - ☐ Bank
    - ☐ Coinage

[Select All] [Clear]

[Save] [Cancel]

Don't forget

As part of your security measures you should change passwords on a regular basis, and especially when a user leaves.

To change a user's password, do the following:

 Select the user, click Edit

 Highlight Password and enter a new one

 Click OK to save, then Save to return to Payroll Desktop

Edit User ✕

Edit User

User Details

Logon Name	Bill
Password	*********

[OK] [Close]

Deleting User Names

You also have the facility to permanently delete a user's details from the Sage Payroll program. You may want to do this, for example, when a payroll user leaves your company.

To delete a user name and their access rights, do the following:

 From the menu bar, click Tasks, then Security and Access Rights... to bring up the Access Rights window

 Select the user whose access details you need to delete from the Users list

 Click on the Delete button

Don't forget

Once a payroll user leaves your company, you should delete their details immediately from the Users list.

Access Rights — □ ×

Users
MANAGER
Bill

[Add] [Edit] [Delete]

Employee Record Access

Weekly	☑	Fortnightly	☑
Four Weekly	☑	Monthly	☑
Access Level	0	Include lower levels	☑

Suppress Non-Essential Messaging

| Employee Record | ☐ | Processing | ☐ |
| Other | ☐ | Automatic Enrolment | ☐ |

Allow Access To These Areas:
- ☑ Personnel Record
  - ☑ Appraisal
  - ☐ Disciplinary
  - ☑ Job History
- ☑ YTD Values
- ☑ P45/P46 Information
- ☑ Leaver
- ☑ Delete Employee
- ☑ Statement of Employment
- ☑ Company
  - ☐ Settings
    - ☐ Details
    - ☐ Bank
    - ☐ Coinage

[Select All] [Clear]

[Save] [Cancel]

Hot tip

If you accidentally select the incorrect user to delete, simply press No when asked to confirm and repeat from Step 2.

4 Click Yes to confirm you want to delete the user, else No to cancel

5 Click Save to record the changes

Sage Payroll ×

❓ Are you sure you want to delete user : Bill?

[Yes] [No]

Beware

If you don't click Save on the Access Rights screen when finished, your changes will NOT be saved. If you click Cancel, you are reminded that changes have been made and asked if you wish to save them.

Passwords

Sage provides you with two levels of security password for using the Payroll program. Firstly, the System Manager can set up a personal password for each user. This is the user's personal password and can be changed by the user as and when required.

The second option involves the setting up of a program password by the Manager. All users must enter this password to gain access to the Payroll program irrespective of whether they have their own personal password or not.

To change the program password

1 From the menu bar, click Tasks, then Security and Change Program Password...

2 Enter the existing password or leave blank if none is set up

3 Enter your new password

4 Re-enter your new password to confirm, and click OK

Change Password		×
Old Password	**********	
New Password	**********	
Confirm New Password	**********	
OK	Cancel	Help

To change your personal password

1 Click Tasks, Security then Change Personal Password...

2 Enter your new password

3 Re-enter your new password to confirm

4 Click OK

Change Personal Password		×
Logon Name	Bill	
New Password	*******	
Confirm New Password	*******	
OK	Cancel	Help

3 Company Settings

Quickly configure all your company defaults before you start using the program. This includes company and bank details, holiday and pension schemes and pay elements.

Entering Company Settings

Before you can start using Sage 50 Payroll for the first time you must enter your company defaults. These include details such as your name, address, tax office, bank, coinage and department details. Company holiday and absence schemes need recording too, as well as any pension schemes you may have.

Don't forget

With Historical Data you can keep a history from the previous seven years of processing.

1 Click on Tasks on the menu bar

2 Select Company, then click on Settings...

3 The Company Settings window appears

4 Enter your company details here

Hot tip

Use the Tab key to quickly move to the next row or input box. Pressing Shift + Tab moves you to the previous row or input.

32

Name	Wizard Training Limited
Address	Wizard House, 10 High Street, Anytown, Anyshire
Post Code	AA1 2ZZ
Telephone	0111 234 5678
Facsimile	0111 234 5679
E-Mail	training@wiztrain.com
Tax Off. Name	Anytown One
Tax Dist./Ref.	123 / 1234567
ECON	3999999R
Employer Ref (CSA/CMEC)	

Male Retirement Age 65
Female Retirement Age 65
Cash Rounding Amount 0.00
Store Historical Data (Years) 7

Eligible for Small Employers' Relief for 2016/17 ☐
Add absence comment ☑
Old style Absence Diary ☐
Show Zero Values on Payslip ☑
Update Absence Diary Automatically ☐
Auto Advance Net to Gross Employees ☐
Clear Enter Payment Notes on Update Records ☐
Use Old Style SSP Entry in Enter Payments ☐
Eligible for Employment Allowance ☐
Operate net of foreign tax credit relief ☐

5 Check and amend any of these defaults if necessary

6 Click OK to save your company details and close the Company Settings window

Don't forget

Whilst entering your company details, remember to also check that your SSP patterns are correctly set up.

Normally, the default settings will not need altering, but if necessary, they can be easily amended. The following explains what the various settings refer to:

Retirement Age:
Although set by default, this can be amended to show any age between 50 and 70, should the need arise through a change in Government legislation.

Cash Rounding Amount:
For employees paid by cash, you can enter here whether to round the payment up or down to the nearest multiple.

Store Historical Data:
You can specify how many years you want to store historical data for. One year is the minimum, seven years is the maximum.

Eligible for Small Employers' Relief:
Tick this box if your company qualifies for the Small Employers' Relief (SER) scheme. If unsure, contact HMRC for scheme details.

Add absence comment:
If this box is ticked, Payroll allows you to include comments on the absence diary.

Old style Absence Diary:
Should you be familiar with previous versions of Sage Payroll and prefer to view the absence diary in the earlier style, simply tick here.

Show Zero Values on Payslip:
A tick here allows values that are zero to appear and be printed on your employees' payslips, otherwise if you prefer, the appropriate spaces will be left blank.

Update Absence Diary Automatically:
Automatically adds holiday or maternity days taken, up to and including the processing date.

Auto Advance Net to Gross Employees (Sage Professional users only):
Tick if you want the Net Payment the employee normally receives to automatically carry through to Advance Payments when advancing holiday pay. This saves having to re-enter the Net Payment in the Advance Pay option later.

You can enter either a negative or positive value between -10.00 and +10.00 for the Cash Rounding Amount. A negative value rounds the employee's pay down to the nearest multiple, whilst a positive number rounds up to the nearest multiple.

To qualify for the Small Employers' Relief (SER) scheme, your total Class 1 NICs must be at or below the HMRC annual threshold in the qualifying tax year.

Company Bank Details

The Bank tab from the Company Settings window allows you to set up your company's bank details. This is necessary as Sage 50 Payroll will use this information when printing cheque and giro details. After opening the Company Settings window, enter your company bank details as follows:

An International Bank Account Number (IBAN) must be used when payments are made or received across country borders in the EU, EEA and Switzerland and is always used in conjunction with a BIC.

1   Click on the Bank tab

2   Enter the bank name in the appropriate field

3   Enter the bank address and other contact details

4   Click here and choose the Account Type

The Bank Identifier Code (BIC) is a standard identifier for banks and should be used on all international payments.

Company Settings ✕

Details | **Bank** | Coinage | Absence | Analysis | Tax Funding | Statutory Funding | HMRC Payments | Documents

Bank Details

Bank	Wizard Bank	Account Type	Bank Account
Address	4 The High Street / Anytown / Anyshire	B/Soc. Roll No.	
		Account Name	Wizard Training Limited
		Account Number	12345678
Post Code	HS1 4GH	Sort Code	11-22-33
Telephone	0111 234 7788	IBAN	
Fax	0111 234 7789	BIC	
Email	info@wizardbank.co.uk	BACS Reference	12312312

Use this account for HMRC refunds in the EPS ☐

E-Banking What is this?

Enable e-Banking ☐   Component [   ] Config

OK   Cancel   Help

5   Enter the rest of your account details

6   If you make or receive payments to or from countries in the European Union, European Economic Areas and Switzerland, you will have an IBAN and BIC to enter

If you pay your employees' wages by automatic credit transfer, enter your company's BACS reference in the box provided. This reference is issued by your bank.

7   Enter your BACS Reference if you have one

8   When finished, click OK to save changes

Coinage Requirements

This facility enables you to set up a minimum quantity of notes and coins that you would like to use when paying your employees in cash. You can also exclude specific notes and coins used in payment calculations.

After opening the Company Settings window, set up the minimum coinage quantities as follows:

 1 Click on the Coinage tab

2 Enter the minimum number of each type of note required in the Pounds Minimum Quantity field

3 Enter the minimum number of each type of coin required in the Pence Minimum Quantity field

Company Settings   ×

| Details | Bank | Coinage | Absence | Analysis | Tax Funding | Statutory Funding | HMRC Payments | Documents |

Pounds

Value in Pounds	Minimum Quantity	Include in Analysis
50	0	Yes
20	5	Yes
10	8	Yes
5	8	Yes
2	15	Yes
1	20	Yes

Pence

Value in Pence	Minimum Quantity	Include in Analysis
50	3	Yes
20	5	Yes
10	2	Yes
5	4	Yes
2	4	Yes
1	2	Yes

OK   Cancel   Help

4 If you don't want to include specific bank note or coinage requirements in the payment calculations, select No in the respective Include in Analysis columns

5 When finished, click OK to save or Cancel to abandon your changes

If your company operates a pension scheme, set up your software so that the pension contributions are automatically deducted when your employees are paid.

Company Pension Schemes

Types of pensions

When all employed earners reach retirement age, they are entitled to receive the Basic State Pension. Employees who have paid Class 1 NI contributions used to be entitled to an additional State Pension, but these rules have now been superceded. The new State Pension is a regular payment from the government for those who reach State Pension age on or after 6 April 2016.

However, employers are now expected to offer their employees the opportunity to join a company or occupational pension scheme, (also called a workplace pension). These schemes provide much better benefits on retirement than the State's basic pension.

Deciding to join an employer's occupational pension scheme was called 'contracting out' of the additional State Pension scheme. When an employee joined the scheme, both they and the employer paid lower, reduced rate NI contributions. When the employee retired, their second pension would come from the employer's scheme and not from the additional State Pension.

Another option was to contract out with a stakeholder pension or a personal pension, resulting in no reduction of National Insurance contributions. Instead, once a year, HM Revenue & Customs would pay a rebate of National Insurance contributions directly into the employee's pension in order to provide benefits broadly the same as the additional State Pension given up.

However, from April 2012 the rules for contracting out changed. Contracting out is not now possible through a stakeholder or personal pension scheme and any employee who has done so will be brought back into the additional State Pension. The employee can continue making their own contributions to the scheme, but with loss of rebate, etc.

Employees contributing to an occupational scheme

Where an employer does provide a scheme, contracting out through an occupational salary related (defined benefit) scheme is still allowed. However, contracting out for these schemes will be reviewed in the future so make sure you keep up-to-date with any proposed changes by regularly visiting the **www.gov.uk** website and checking the Working, Jobs and Pensions pages. Contracting out through a money purchase (defined contribution) occupational pension scheme has also stopped.

Making payments

Contributions made from the employee's pay into the pension scheme must be deducted from the employee's gross pay before calculating the tax due on the pay. This is known as a 'net pay arrangement'. Where an employee decides to pay AVCs into the pension scheme, these are treated the same way as the pension contributions and are also deducted from gross pay before any tax is calculated.

Contracting out

As stated, some occupational pension schemes contracted out of the additional State Pension scheme. For these schemes, both the employees who were members and the employer paid a reduced rate of NIC. The lower rate of National Insurance payable was the 'D' rate.

Because you can't contract out after 6 April 2016, the National Insurance 'D' rate no longer exists. If an employee was contracted out, their National Insurance contributions increase to the standard rate from this date. 'A' rate is the standard class of National Insurance payable for employees.

Getting started pension checklist

Before entering your pension, work through this checklist:

- Which scheme – fixed amount or percentage?
- Is the pension paid on all elements amounting to gross or just on certain payments?
- If a percentage, does this apply to the employee's total earnings?
- Does the pension scheme have a minimum contribution per pay period or a maximum yearly contribution?
- For NIC purposes do you require your pension figure to be calculated between the Lower and Upper Earnings Limit?
- Do you wish to include in your pension calculation SSP and SMP payments?
- Does tax relief apply to your pension amount?

Additional Voluntary Contributions (AVCs) are used to top up a shortfall or gaps in an employee's National Insurance contributions record. Time limits and conditions apply.

Use the HMRC website, **www.hmrc.gov.uk** if you have any queries relating to pension contribution calculations.

If you have queries regarding pension contributions, check with your pension adviser BEFORE setting up your pension details.

A salary sacrifice pension scheme is set up differently in your Sage software. Please read the information in Chapter 11 for details of how to do this.

...cont'd

To set up your company pension scheme details

You need to record the details of any company pension scheme so that Sage 50 Payroll can then automatically calculate the appropriate pension contributions. To set up your company pension scheme details, do the following:

 Click on Tasks on the menu bar

2 Select Company, then click on Pension Schemes...

3 Click New in the Pension Schemes window

4 Enter a new pension scheme Reference here

You need to enter pension information for both employee and employer contributions.

38

Pension

Details | Employee | Employer | Provider

Scheme Details

Reference: 11
Description:
Type: Other
SCON:
Qualifying Scheme ☐
Use Qualifying Earnings for pensionable pay ☐
Scheme minimum contribution (Total of Ee and Er): 0.00
Minimum Employment Period (Months): 0
Salary Sacrifice Scheme ☐

 Type a Description for your pension scheme

6 Select the pension type from the drop-down list in the Type field, then complete the rest of the details

7 Use the tabs to enter Employee, Employer and Provider details and click OK to save when done

Refer to Chapter 11 for more detailed information on pension schemes and how to edit an existing scheme.

Additional notes on entering your company pension scheme details

In the Contribution Details area you need to select either Percentage or Fixed Amount from the drop-down list for both employer and employee, then enter the value of the percentage or amount in the next box.

If a percentage scheme is in use, you need to select one of the following options so that Sage 50 Payroll knows how to calculate the percentage contribution:

Apply to all Pensionable Earnings:	This applies the percentage to the employee's total earnings.
Restrict to Statutory N.I. Upper/Lower Bands:	Check this option to apply the pension percentage to the NI earnings bands only.
Restrict to specific Upper/Lower Bands:	This will apply the percentage to the limits specified by you in the Upper and Lower limits boxes which appear when you select this option.

Other scheme details you can specify are:

Calculate Minimum Rebate:	This depends on the scheme selected. If checked, it calculates the NI contracted out rebate. Untick if not applicable.
Include Rebate and Amount:	Select to total the percentage and minimum rebate values.
Include SSP Payments:	If selected, Payroll includes any SSP payments in the total pensionable pay.
Include SMP, SAP or SPP Payments:	If any selected, Payroll includes the SMP, SAP or SPP payments in the total pensionable pay.
Deduct Before Tax:	If ticked, this allows tax relief on pension contributions. Deducts payments from gross before tax.

Use the Calculator button to quickly enter an amount or fixed percentage figure.

The availability of the Include Rebate and Amount check box depends on the type of scheme selected.

For the Deduct Before Tax option, legislation determines which types of schemes allow contributions to be deducted before tax. This means that the box is always shaded unless you choose Other from the Type drop-down list in the Details tab.

Company Holiday Schemes

Your company's holiday and absence scheme details also need setting up. The start date of your holiday and absence year needs recording, together with the statutory sickness payment qualifying patterns. To enter this information, do the following:

Hot tip

Sage 50 Payroll has a number of holiday schemes already set up for you to edit as required.

Hot tip

Use the National Holidays tab to quickly view a list of statutory bank holiday dates for a particular year.

Don't forget

If a new starter begins halfway through the pay period and you wish to accrue holiday for the full period, select the Include Starting Pay Month check box.

1 Click on Tasks on the menu bar

2 Select Company, then click on Holidays...

3 In the Holidays window, select the first scheme and click Edit

4 Type your Scheme Name and amend the number of entitlement days if necessary

Holiday Schemes - Edit Scheme 1

Scheme Number   1   Scheme Name   Holiday Scheme : 1

Entitlement Settings   Payments

Basis
Scheme Type   ⦿ Specified Entitlement   ○ Calculated Entitlement
Entitlement of   30.0   Days

Accrual
Accrue Holiday   Daily
Display Excess Entitlement Warning   ☑

Settings
Include National Holidays in Entitlement   ☐ Minimum Employment (Months)   0
Allow Entitlement B/F From Previous Year   ☑ Allow Entitlement Advanced From Next Year   ☐
Include Starting Pay Month   ☐ Include Current Pay Month

OK   Cancel   Help

5 Select how the holiday entitlement is to accrue, either Daily or Calendar Monthly, from the drop-down list

6 Complete the remaining settings as appropriate, then click OK to save or Cancel to abandon

Additional notes on setting up your company holiday schemes

The Sage 50 Payroll Holiday window tabs offer a number of options which allow you to exactly tailor each holiday scheme your company operates. The remaining options not covered on the previous page are as follows:

Allow Entitlement B/F From Previous Year:	Allows holiday not taken during the year to be carried forward and added to next year's entitlement.
Allow Entitlement Advanced From Next Year:	Allows an employee to take holiday entitlement from next year, if agreed with your company.
Include Starting Pay Month:	Where a new starter joins the company half way through the current pay period, a tick in this box allows holiday to be accrued for the full period.
Include Current Pay Month:	Where an employee's payroll is processed part way through a period but you want to accrue holiday for the full period, simply tick here.
Display Excess Entitlement Warning:	Displays a warning whenever an employee exceeds their holiday entitlement.

Working Day Patterns

You can also set up a number of Working Day Patterns for an employee, e.g. where someone works shift patterns that change on a weekly basis. This is done via the Holiday Schemes Settings tab:

1 Click in the Working Day Pattern box

Ref	Sun to Sat Pattern
4	NQQQNNN
5	NQQQQNN
6	QNNNNNQ
7	QNQNQNQ
8	NQNQNQN

OK   Close

2 Click on the Finder button

3 Select an appropriate pattern and click OK

Abbreviations to remember when entering Holiday Scheme Patterns:

Q = Qualifying

N = Non-qualifying

The Pattern Start Date must run from Sunday to Saturday, so a normal five day working week (Monday to Friday) would be:

NQQQQQN

41

For a handy PDF guide to setting up holiday schemes, simply press F1 when in the Holidays window and click 'Read the full guide' or on the PDF icon under the heading Dealing with employees' holidays.

Departments and Cost Centres

Should you want to, a large number of Departments and Cost Centres can be easily set up in Sage 50 Payroll and then allocated to each employee. To set up your Departments and Cost Centres, after opening the Company Settings window, do the following:

To view or print Cost Centre and Departmental Analysis information, click Reports on the menu bar, then select the Employee folder.

1 Click on the Analysis tab

2 The Analysis tab window displays any Departments and Cost Centres already set up

3 Click here and enter a new Department name

Hot tip

To delete a department from the list, simply select it and press the Delete button on your keyboard, then press Tab to accept the changes.

Company Settings   ×

| Details | Bank | Coinage | Absence | Analysis | Tax Funding | Statutory Funding | HMRC Payments | Documents |

Departments

Ref.	Name
1	Directors
2	Management
3	Sales
4	Administration
5	Analysts
6	Programmers
7	[unnamed department]

Cost Centres

Ref.	Name
ACC	Accounts
PAY	Payroll

Employee Analysis

Analysis 1	Analysis 2	Analysis 3
Union Member	Job Title	Analysis3

OK   Cancel   Help

Beware

You cannot delete a department whilst you still have employees assigned to it.

4 Press the keyboard Tab key to accept the entry

5 To create a new cost centre, use the Cost Centres box and repeat Steps 3 and 4

6 To edit a Department or Cost Centre name, simply click on the one you wish to change and type a new name

7 When you have finished making your changes, click OK to save or Cancel to abandon

Pay Elements

The Pay Elements option is where payment, deduction and loan types are set up. You will find that Attachments have already been set up for you. Pay Elements need setting up before you enter your employee details, after which the payment and deduction types can be applied to each individual.

Sage 50 Payroll lets you create an unlimited number of payment, deduction and loan types. Payments are divided into four types, namely factor, global, fixed and variable. For global payment types, any changes to the payment elements will affect all employees assigned to them, whereas for fixed payment types, the rate/amount is fixed by the value entered in each individual Employee Record. Variable payment types allow the user more flexibility in recording changes to rates or hours. To set up payment types:

Hot tip

Use the Edit button when you need to make changes to any payments, deductions or loans details.

1 Click on Tasks, Company and select Pay Elements...

2 The Pay Elements Settings window appears

Pay Elements Settings

Tabs: Payments | Deductions | Loans | Attachment of Earnings Orders | Net Payments | Salary Sacrifice

Ref	Description	Status	Hours/No	Rate
1	Salary	Variable	35.0000	0.0000
2	Commission	Fixed	0.0000	15.0000
3	Bonus	Global	1.0000	100.0000
4	Expenses	Variable	1.0000	0.0000
5	Overtime	Variable	0.0000	0.0000
6	Net Salary	Variable	1.0000	950.0000

Buttons: New | Edit | Delete | Batch Factor

OK | Close | Help

Hot tip

You can also use the Employee Wizard from the Wizards menu to help you assign payments, deduction and loan types to an employee from the start of their employment.

3 To add a new payment type, click on the New button

...cont'd

Hot tip

Simply enter a default number of hours for Default Hours/No to save time later when processing, otherwise each employee's Payments tab will need individually updating.

Hot tip

Unless all your employees receive the same rate of pay, it is advisable to initially leave the default Rate as zero.

Don't forget

Auto Advance uses the last updated pay period values to advance holiday pay.

4 Click here and select Status type from the drop-down list

5 Enter payment Description

6 Enter Default Number of Hours

New Payment ✕

Reference	7	Status	Variable ▼
Description *		Base Payment	Factor
			Fixed
Default Hours/No.	0.0000		Global
Rate	0.0000		**Variable**

This payment is subject to:

PAYE	☑	Qualifying Earnings	☑	⑦ Community Charge	☑
National Insurance	☑	Pension (Main)	☑	Council Tax	☑
Salary Sacrifice (Pension Only)	☐	Pension (AVC)	☑	Other Attachments	☑
				Benefit in Kind	☐

Include Value in Minimum/Living Wage calculation ☑

Include Hours/No in Minimum/Living Wage calculation ☑

This payment includes premium element ☐

| Include for Holiday Accrual | ☑ | Include for Weekly Averages | ☑ |
| Auto Advance | ☐ | Include in Timesheet Entry | ☑ |

[Batch Factor]   [OK]   [Close]   [Help]

---

7 Enter an initial Rate only if necessary

8 Tick all the various options that are relevant to this pay element, then click OK to save, or Close to abandon

9 To edit a payment, select it from the list then click the Edit button and follow Steps 4 to 8 above

4 The Nominal Link

Setting up the Nominal Link

To transfer your payroll information directly to the nominal ledger of your Sage accounts program, it is important to set up the Nominal Settings before processing your first payroll. To set up the Nominal Settings, do the following:

1 Click on Tasks on the menu bar

2 Select Company, then click on Nominal Settings...

3 The Nominal Link Settings window appears

4 Click here and select Destination from the drop-down list

You can post your payroll data directly into the following accounts software:

- Sage 50 Accounts
- Sage Instant Accounts
- Sage 200 Accounts
- TAS BOOKS v8 or lower
- TASBooks v1 or above
- a File for importing into other software

5 Use the Browse... button to find the path to your Company File

6 Select Company if more than one and click OK to save

Setting up Nominal Codes

Default nominal codes are already set up by Sage but if you use different Company nominal codes these will need setting up before posting your payroll information. To enter your own Profit & Loss (P&L) and Balance Sheet (BS) nominal codes, do this:

Profit & Loss

1 From the Nominal Link Settings window select the P&L Analysis tab

2 Check the various nominal codes, add or edit as necessary

Profit and Loss Category	Acc N/C	Acc C/C	Acc Dept
Attachments Admin Fee	7000		
Deductions	7000		
Employers NIC	7006		
Employers Pension	7007		
Payments	7000		
SAP	7011		
SAP Recovered	7000		
ShPP			
ShPP Recovered			
SMP	7011		
SMP Recovered	7000		
SPP	7011		
SPP Recovered	7000		
SSP	7010		

3 Click Close when finished to save any changes

Balance Sheet

1 From the Nominal Link Settings window select the BS Analysis tab

2 Check the various nominal codes and edit as necessary

Balance Sheet Category	Acc N/C	Acc C/C	Acc Dept
Attachments	9999		
Holiday Fund	2240		
Loan Repayments	9998		
National Insurance	2211		
Net Wages	2220		
PAYE	2210		
Pension	2230		
Student Loan	9998		

Bank Payment N/C 1200

3 Select the nominal code for the bank you pay your employee's wages from in the Bank Payment N/C field

4 Click OK when finished to save any changes

(See pages 48-50 for details of how to set up override facilities for any of the above settings.)

Beware

The codes entered in the P&L Analysis and BS Analysis windows must exist in your accounts program, otherwise Payroll will display a warning message that any postings to these codes will be sent to Mispostings (9999).

Hot tip

For analysis purposes, Sage 50 Payroll users can record an account cost centre (Acc. C/C) and an accounts department (Acc. Dept) against each nominal code.

Payments Override

There are different types of Override options, such as for Payments, Deductions, Pensions, Departmental, etc. This lets you separate the nominal code categories used in order to produce a more detailed analysis of your costs. You may, for example, wish to separate your payments into their individual parts, such as salary, overtime or bonus, and post the details to specific nominal codes. Different accounts departments can also be set up against each individual element.

1 From the P&L Analysis tab, click Payments Override

2 Click here to bring up the payment types you can override

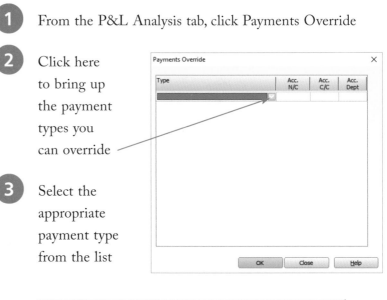

3 Select the appropriate payment type from the list

Ref	Name	Tax	NI
-2	Salary	Pre	Pre
1	Salary	Pre	Pre
2	Commission	Pre	Pre
3	Bonus	Pre	Pre
4	Expenses	Post	Post

4 Click OK

5 Back in the Payments Override window, enter the nominal code (Acc. N/C), cost centre (Acc. C/C) and department (Acc. Dept) you wish to use, as applicable

6 Click OK to store details or Close to abandon changes

Deductions/Pensions Override

Deductions can either be a Profit & Loss or Balance Sheet nominal code (see page 47). To allow a more detailed analysis of your deductions payments, follow the steps below:

1 From the P&L Analysis tab click Deductions Override

2 Click here to bring up the deduction types you can override

3 Select the appropriate deduction from the list and click OK

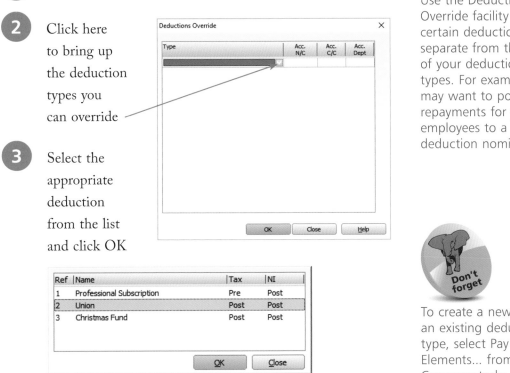

4 In the Deductions Override window, enter the nominal code (Acc. N/C), cost centre (Acc. C/C) and department (Acc. Dept) you wish to use, then click OK

Pensions Override

1 From the P&L Analysis tab click Pensions Override

2 Do Steps 2 to 4 above to set up any Pensions Overrides

Hot tip

Use the Deductions Override facility to keep certain deductions separate from the rest of your deduction types. For example, you may want to post car repayments for your employees to a separate deduction nominal code.

Don't forget

To create a new or edit an existing deduction type, select Pay Elements... from the Company tasks, then the Deductions tab.

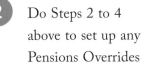

Hot tip

Pensions Overrides can be set up from either the P&L Analysis or BS Analysis screens.

Departmental Override

Sage 50 Payroll provides you with the facility to set up and analyse your payments and deductions by Department. The example below shows you, using customised nominal codes, how to select the Sales department and post employees' wages to a different nominal code from their overtime payments. This information will then be used within the Profit & Loss report.

 From either the P&L Analysis or BS Analysis tabs, click the Departmental Override button

 Select the department required here and click Edit

 Enter your additional nominal codes in the Acc. N/C column

 Click Payments Override

 Click in the Type column and select your payment type from the list

 Enter the payment type nominal code in the Acc. N/C column

 Repeat Steps 5-6 as required

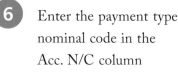

 Click OK and OK again, note 'Yes' in the Override column, then click Close

Nominal Link Postings

Once you have updated your payroll, the Nominal Link Wizard will guide you through processing your payroll postings. It is important, however, to back up your accounts data first before carrying out this procedure.

1 Make a backup of your accounts data file

2 Click Wizards on the menu bar and select Nominal Link

Let the Nominal Link Wizard take you through posting your payroll payments directly to your accounts program.

3 The Nominal Link Wizard starts, click Next to continue

4 Select the process date you require and click Next

Remember that Nominal Link postings can only be made after the payroll has been updated.

5 Check the details are correct. Cancel if you need to make changes, else click Next

6 Enter a Transaction Reference and check details in the window showing which options will be used for your postings

7 If not required, untick Group Transactions then click Next

The Nominal Link can only post one payment type at a time, i.e. monthly, weekly.

...cont'd

 8 Click Print for a paper copy of the postings in case you need to check anything later

 Always print a list of payroll transactions for checking purposes before updating your accounts package.

9 Click Finish to post the Bank Payments

10 The Nominal Link Wizard prepares the transactions for posting and checks access to Sage Accounts. The Logon window appears when the link has been established

 You must make sure there are no errors because once you have clicked Finish, the transactions will be added to the audit trail within your Sage Accounts package.

11 Enter the Logon details for your Sage Accounts and click OK to post Nominal Transactions

12 When the Nominal Link Wizard has finished posting your transactions, details of postings are shown and a confirmation appears

 Always ensure that postings have been made correctly by checking through the audit trail of your Sage Accounts program.

13 Click OK to close the Nominal Link Wizard

5 Employee Records

This chapter explains how to set up and maintain your employees' personal records and keep track of their payments. This includes items such as tax codes, rates of pay, bank account and absence information. These details will then be used automatically during payroll processing.

Form P46 has now been replaced by the Starter Checklist, which contains the same information. For simplicity, because Sage 50 Payroll still refers to form P46, so does this book.

For speed, on the main Payroll Desktop simply click the right mouse button for a list of tasks when dealing with your employees' records.

You can now record if a new employee is disabled, an apprentice, or a non-UK worker together with their passport number in the Employee Wizard.

Creating Employee Records

When setting up new Employee Records, use the Employee Wizard to help you enter the majority of your employee payroll details, for example, personal, bank and payment details. Certain information is essential and must be entered, i.e. Surname, Tax Code, NI Number, Date of Birth, Start Date, etc.

Where employees have joined your organisation part way through the tax year, cumulative figures from their previous employment need to be entered. These figures, gathered from the employee's P45, are entered into the Taxable Gross Pay and Total Tax Paid boxes. If an employee does not supply a P45, then they must complete a Starter Checklist. The Wizard will detail necessary instructions to successfully complete your payroll information.

New Employee Records can be created at any time. Additional information can be entered, or amendments made, using the Employee Record button from the Payroll toolbar.

To set up a new Employee Record, do the following:

 From the Wizards menu select Employee Wizard...

 Make sure you have all of the information to hand and click Next to progress through the Wizard screens and enter your new employee details

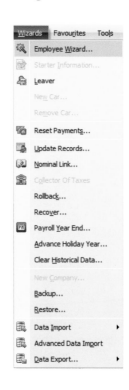

Employee Wizard

Welcome to the Employee Wizard.
This wizard helps you to enter new employee information.

⊙ Record the details of a new starter using their starter form

The following options require an employee to be selected from the desktop

○ Create an employee record based on an existing employee

○ Re-employ an employee

Certain fields are compulsory. These are marked with the symbol *

| Cancel | < Back | Next > | Finish |

3 Check the Reference no. is correct and edit if necessary

4 Enter employee's name and address details, use the drop-down list where provided

Employee Wizard

Reference *	26
Works Number	26
Title *	Mr
Surname *	Mr.
Forenames *	Mrs.
	Miss.
Address	Ms.
	Dr.
	Sir
Post Code	Country United Kingdom
Home Tel	
Mobile Tel	

Cancel   < Back   Next >   Finish

All fields marked with the asterisk symbol '*' must be completed. You cannot proceed to the next screen until you have done so.

5 Click Next to continue

6 Enter compulsory information for the first four fields, noting that depending on the selected Title in the previous screen, some fields have been completed for you

7 Complete rest of the fields with the relevant details

Employee Wizard

Sex *	Female
Marital Status *	Married
Date of Birth *	20/12/1987 Disabled ☐
Employee Start Date *	05/12/2016 Apprentice ☐
Job Title	
Passport Number	
Nationality	
Ethnic Origin	Non-UK Worker ☐
RTI Payroll ID	8DD896E512B9974A Edit

Cancel   < Back   Next >   Finish

8 Click Next

9 Select P45 or the relevant P46 as appropriate

RTI Payroll ID is a unique value used by HMRC to identify employees when you make submissions. If changing from another payroll system, click Edit and enter the existing ID or specify that it is unknown or not set. You cannot amend this once the record is created.

10 Alternatively, click here if this is an existing employee

Employee Wizard

Which form has your new starter provided?

P45
None, existing employee
P45
P46
P46(Expat)
P46(Pen)

Is your employee in the Government's Welfare To Work programme? ☐

Cancel   < Back   Next >   Finish

11 Tick if your employee is in the Welfare to Work scheme, then click Next

Previous employment P45 details may be entered using the YTD Values option from the Employee task list.

...cont'd

Don't forget

Check which statement the employee has completed on their P45 or P46 form and select the correct Declaration from the drop-down list.

Don't forget

A National Insurance number must start with two alphabetical characters followed by six numbers and a final letter in the range A-D, for example, NW 12 34 56 A.

Hot tip

If an employee's NI number is not known, Sage will generate a temporary one; just click Yes when prompted.

 Enter previous employment tax details

 Enter if Student Loan is applicable

 Click Next

 Enter your employee's NI details or tick if Not Known

Employee Wizard

Enter the tax details relating to the employee's previous employment within the current tax year.

Starting Declaration *	Statement A
Previous Employment Tax Dist./Ref.	123 / 4567890123
Date Left Previous Employment	02/12/2016
Tax Code at Leaving Date *	1100L
Was this on a Week 1/Month 1 basis?	No
Total Pay to Date	0.00
Total Tax to Date	0.00
Continue Student Loan Deductions?	No

Cancel   < Back   Next >   Finish

Employee Wizard

Enter your employee's National Insurance information.

If you do not know their National Insurance number, a temporary number will be automatically generated. Do you know this employee's National Insurance Number?

Contact your local Tax Office for details on how to obtain the correct National Insurance number as soon as possible.

National Insurance Number *	☐ Not Known AB 123456 C
National Insurance Category *	A

Cancel   < Back   Next >   Finish

16 Click Next to continue

17 Select how you want to process payments to this employee

18 Enter Holiday and Pension Scheme details, then click Next

Employee Wizard

Payment Method	BACS
Payment Frequency	Monthly
Gross Salary	0.0000 per Month
Is this employee a director?	Non-Director
Holiday Scheme	1
Pension Scheme	1
Department	
Cost Centre	

Cancel   < Back   Next >   Finish

 Choose the type of payment required from the drop-down list or create a New Payment

 Click Next to continue

Employee Wizard

What types of payment do you want to allocate to your employee?

Payment Name	Hours/No.	Rate
Salary	35.0000	0.0000

Create a   New Payment   New Net Payment

Apply Minimum/Living Wage check ☐

Cancel   < Back   Next >   Finish

21 Choose your deduction type, e.g. Union, from the drop-down list or click New Deduction

Employee Wizard

What types of deduction do you want to allocate to your employee?

Deduction Name	Hours/No.	Rate
Union	0.0000	14.7800

Create a [New Deduction]

[Cancel]   [< Back] [Next >]   [Finish]

22 Click Next to continue

23 Select Account Type and enter the relevant details

Employee Wizard

Enter your employee's bank or building society branch details.

Account Type   [Bank Account]
Bank
Address

Post Code

[Cancel]   [< Back] [Next >]   [Finish]

24 Click Next

25 In the next screen, enter the employee's bank account details

Employee Wizard

Enter your employee's bank account details.

Account Name   [|]
Account Number [ ]
Sort Code   [00-00-00]

If you pay your employee using BACS or Automated Credit Transfer, enter the unique reference code below:

BACS/ACT Reference [ ]

[Cancel]   [< Back] [Next >]   [Finish]

57

26 Enter a BACS or ACT Reference if applicable

27 Click Next

28 Click Finish to save the information you have just entered, else click Back to make a change

Employee Wizard

You have entered the information needed for your new employee.

Click Back to change any of the details entered on a previous page, or click Finish to create the employee record and complete the Employee Wizard.

[Cancel]   [< Back] [Next >]   [Finish]

The Bank Account Number requires an eight-digit value. Where an account is less than eight digits, just use leading zeros.

Quick Employee Records

This method speeds up the process of creating new Employee Records by allowing you to enter all the basic employee information in one go, namely: personal details, bank, tax, national insurance and pay details. To add more information to an employee's record you then need to follow some of the steps shown on page 59. To initially set up the basic information for a new employee, do the following:

Hot tip

From the Sage 50 Payroll Desktop you can select and open an Employee Record simply by double clicking on the appropriate record.

1 Click on Tasks on the menu bar

2 Select Employee, then click on Quick Employee...

3 Enter Employee's personal details, using the drop-down lists where available

Hot tip

To process a batch of employees with similar details, click the Save & Retain button to keep some of the information onscreen.

4 Enter payment information and bank account details

5 Complete pay details, click Save & Clear, then Close

58

Editing Employee Records

Once your Employee Records have been created using the Employee Wizard or Quick Employee, you can update/edit their existing records as follows:

1 From the Employee List, double-click the employee you wish to edit

2 Using the Personal tab, enter or edit employee details

3 You can also enter appraisal or disciplinary information using the Personnel button on the toolbar

4 Click here to insert a bitmap (*.bmp) picture of the employee

Don't forget

You cannot edit the employee's reference number. It is a unique number generated sequentially by the Payroll program.

Hot tip

From the toolbar, use the Clear and Swap buttons to quickly select or deselect Employee Records.

59

Employee Record - Ref: 18 - Mr. Gavin Maxwell	— □ ×

Toolbar: New | Starter Form | Personnel | First | Previous | Next | Last | Add Photo

Tabs: Personal | Employment | Pensions | Absence | Cars/Fuel | Banking | Analysis | History | Terms | Documents

Reference *	18	Sex	Male
Title *	Mr.	Initials	G	Marital Status	Single
Surname *	Maxwell	Previous Surname	
Forenames *	Gavin	Date of Birth *	18/02/1970
Address	51 Killyworth Road Killingworth Newcastle	Age	46
		Disabled	☑
Post Code	NE12 34A	Nationality	British
Country	United Kingdom	Ethnic Origin	White European
Telephone	0191 26264111	Passport Number	
Mobile			
E-Mail			

* denotes a compulsory field

Emergency Contacts | Personal Cars

Save | Close

5 When finished making changes, click Save to record the employee's personal details or Close to abandon the changes and start again if necessary

Hot tip

Click on the P45/P46 button on the Employee Record toolbar to quickly access the P45/P46 Information Wizard.

Hot tip

Use the drop-down list in the Employment Type entry box to quickly select the employee's employment status, for example, Temporary or Full time.

Beware

It is recommended that you do not change an employee's pay frequency part way through a pay period.

Don't forget

For an existing employee, you should make student loan deductions if HMRC sends you a Start Notice form, SL1.

...cont'd

When an employee's employment details change, for example, a change of tax code, the details can be amended as follows:

 From the Employee Record click the Employment tab

 Add a Job Title if appropriate

 Click here to enter a new Tax Code

Employee Record - Ref: 18 - Mr. Gavin Maxwell — ☐ ✕

New | Starter Form | Personnel | First | Previous | Next | Last | Add Photo

Personal | **Employment** | Pensions | Absence | Cars/Fuel | Banking | Analysis | History | Terms | Documents

Job Title	
	Works Number 18
	Director Status Non-Director
Tax Code * 810L Week 1/Month 1 Basis ☐	Payment Method Cash
NI Category * A Manual NI Entry ☐	Payment Frequency Four Weekly
N.I. Number * NH 379454 B	Employment Type
Starter Form None	
	Student Loan Start / /
Start Date * 02/01/2002 Welfare To Work ☐	Student Loan Type
Leave Date / / FPS Starter ☐	Student Loan End / /
Status OK Non-UK Worker ☐	Student Loan Priority 0
RTI Payroll ID 9aeb0e49a11647b89dfdf416eb7a2c98	Protected Earnings 0.00
Operate net of foreign tax credit relief ☐	

Pay Elements | Salary | YTD Values | Leaver | Apprentice

Save | Close

 For a new employee, check with HMRC before using the Week 1/Month 1 Basis option

Also for a new employee, if either their P45 has a Y in the Continue Student Loan Deductions box or their P46 has a tick in box D, Student Loans, you should now enter student loan deductions

Check the rest of the details then click Save

Employee Pay Elements

Before processing your payroll, your employees' payment details need setting up. Payments can range from hourly, daily, weekly, to monthly. Where, for example, hours worked per week may vary, these entries can be left blank and set up during the payroll run itself. Follow the steps below to set up your pay elements:

1 From the Employee Record, select the Employment tab

2 Click the Pay Elements button

3 Click here and choose a Payment Name from the list

4 Click OK and repeat as required

5 Pre or Post appears in the Tax and NI columns depending on the payment

6 Enter the number of hours, e.g. 35 hours

7 Enter Rate, e.g. £7.50, and tick to apply the Minimum Wage Check, if necessary

8 Click Save when done

If you enter an incorrect payment type for your employee, select the Payment Name, press F8 and click Yes to delete.

Depending on your version of Payroll program, you can tick Apply Net to Gross Payments to allocate net payments only to the employee. Then, when an employee is processed, click the Net to Gross button on the Enter Payments window to enter the value you wish to pay them.

Entering P45 and YTD Details

The P45 details may be entered for each employee using the YTD Values button from the Employee Record. Use a P46 if taking on a new employee who doesn't have a P45 from a previous employer.

To enter these details, do the following:

1 Click the YTD Values button on the Employment tab

2 Enter the pay and previous employment figures from the employee's P45/P46, such as Gross Pay for Tax and Tax Paid

3 Enter any remaining details as necessary

4 Click OK to Save

Hot tip

Where an employee starts work part way through the tax year, their cumulative tax details may be entered using the Employee Wizard. See page 54.

Don't forget

You will be unable to enter information for fields marked as not applicable (n/a).

62

You can also use the same window if you need to check current pay and tax information for existing employees, as follows:

1 Click the YTD Values button on the Employment tab

2 Previous and current pay and tax details are displayed

3 Any applicable Tax Refunds Withheld are also displayed

4 Make changes if needed

5 When finished, click OK

Hot tip

You can also enter YTD figures by clicking the P45/P46 button from the Employee Record.

NIC

The NIC tab includes detailed information regarding National Insurance contributions paid during the current tax year. To view an employee's NI contributions do the following:

 Click the YTD Values button on the Employment tab and select the NIC tab

2 The NIC window shows details of NI Contributions paid for the current tax year

3 You can edit some entries if relevant

4 Click OK to Save

Payments & Deductions

Year to Date values for an employee's payments and deductions can also be checked, as follows:

1 Click the YTD Values button on the Employment tab and select the Payments & Deductions tab

2 Year to Date Payments and Deductions are displayed for you to check

3 When finished, click OK

To enter an employee's P45 details part way through the current tax year, just use the Tax and NIC tabs.

Always select the employee or employees you require from the Employee List box before viewing or entering any new information.

Refer to Chapter 7 for more information about Payment of Employees.

...cont'd

Refer to Chapter 12 for information about setting up and processing your Attachment of Earnings.

If you start using your Payroll program part way through the tax year, your employees' year to date cumulative totals can be taken from their P11 deduction details.

Once Other YTD figures are entered, they are updated by the system after each payroll run and will be cleared at Year End.

Attachments

This tab shows an employee's Attachment of Earnings payments after all other deductions for tax, pension, NI, etc. have been made. The Order Priority, any protected earnings and admin fee are also displayed here. To check your employee's attachments:

 Click the YTD Values button on the Employment tab and select the Attachments tab

 The Attachments window shows details of any attachments set up for the current tax year

 Use this button to open the drop-down list

 Click OK to exit

Other YTD

You can enter figures directly from your manual records regarding pension contributions, cash rounding carried forward, holiday pay, net pay and loan payments. The example below shows an existing employee's Other YTD information, though Statutory Payments and Director's NIC (where appropriate) can be viewed similarly:

1 Click the YTD Values button on the Employment tab and select the Other YTD tab

2 Details can be viewed or entered here

3 When finished, click OK

Assigning a Holiday Scheme

Once your holiday schemes have been set up using company settings, each employee can be assigned a holiday scheme. You will then be able to record staff holidays, the number of days taken, holidays accrued and notification when holiday entitlement has been exceeded.

To assign a holiday scheme to an employee, do the following:

1 Double-click on required employee in the Employee List

2 From Employee Record click the Absence tab, then the Holiday button

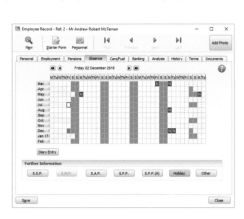

3 In the Holiday window select a scheme if it's different to the default one

4 Select the Entitlement tab to view details of holiday Due and Accrued

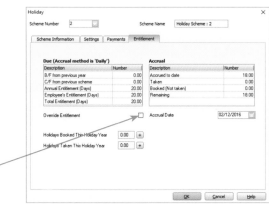

5 Click here to override entitlement if necessary

6 Click on ⊞ for a breakdown of Holidays Booked or Taken, then Close and OK to close the Holiday window

Hot tip

For Qualifying Day Patterns:
N= Non-qualifying
Q= Qualifying

Don't forget

Use the Settings tab, Working Day Pattern box to select a working day pattern for your employee, e.g. for employees working Monday to Friday they would require the pattern NQQQQQN.

Hot tip

For more information about the holiday Accrual Details click the Payments tab.

Recording Employee Holidays

Once a holiday scheme has been set up for an employee, their holiday can be recorded on the Employee Record's Absence tab using the Diary Entry button. To record an employee's holiday, follow the steps below:

1 From the Employee Record select the Absence tab

2 Click on the Diary Entry button

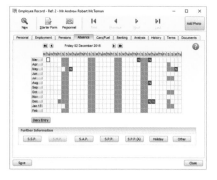

3 Select Holiday from the Absence Type drop-down list

4 On the right of Holiday, select whether holiday is Taken or Booked

5 Select AM or PM to record holiday as a half or full day and enter the dates

6 Enter additional holiday details in the Comment field as necessary

7 Click OK to save holiday details or Cancel to abandon

Remember that you can quickly preview or print a range of Absence or Holiday reports for your employees using the Reports option from the main toolbar.

Recording Sickness

Recording absence through sickness for an employee is recorded using the Diary Entry button on the Absence tab of their Employee Record. Note that the AM/PM option is not available.

To enter your employee's sickness details

1 From the Employee Record, select the Absence tab

2 Click on the Diary Entry button

3 Select SSP from the Absence Type drop-down list

4 On the right of SSP, select the type of absence

5 Enter dates for your employee's absence

Don't forget

Half days are not applicable to SSP.

6 Enter additional absence details in the Comment field as necessary

7 Click OK to save

8 You can also record all types of absence directly from the Absence tab. See the Hot Tip opposite

Hot tip

For more information about SSP for a particular employee just click the S.S.P. button on the Absence tab.

Hot tip

Absences can also be recorded by simply highlighting the dates the employee is absent, then clicking the right mouse button and selecting details using the drop-down lists.

68

Hot tip

Click Other on the Absence tab for a list of absence types and the yearly analysis.

Hot tip

Sage Payroll gives you nine different Custom Absence Types. To give them more suitable names, simply select Tasks from the Payroll toolbar, then the Absence tab from the Company Settings window and edit the Custom Absence Reasons descriptions.

Hot tip

An employee's absence can be viewed quickly using the Absence Diary screen. A fully coloured square indicates one day's absence, whereas a half coloured square reflects a half day's absence, AM or PM.

Custom Types of Absence

Besides recording absence for holidays and sickness, you may have to record absence for medical reasons, paternity leave, etc. Sage Payroll provides a list of absence types for you to choose from. However, to enter a custom type of absence for an employee, follow the steps below:

1 From the Employee Record, select the Absence tab

2 Click the arrows to select the required month and year

3 Click on a square to find the correct date

4 Or, use the mouse to highlight a range of dates as required

5 Click the right mouse button and select an appropriate Custom Absence Type from the drop-down lists

6 Add a Comment if required in the Absence Information window

7 Click OK to save

Employee Bank Details

If you wish to enter your employee's bank/building society details or amend existing information, you can do this by using the Banking tab on the Employee Record. To do this, follow the steps below:

1 Select employee required and click the Banking tab on the Employee Record

2 Enter name of bank and complete the rest of bank details

3 Select Account Type

4 Complete Account Name, Number and Sort Code

B/Soc Roll No. is only needed for building society accounts.

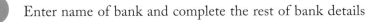

Employee Record - Ref: 2 - Mr Andrew Robert McTernan

| New | Starter Form | Personnel | First | Previous | Next | Last | Add Photo |

Personal | Employment | Pensions | Absence | Cars/Fuel | **Banking** | Analysis | History | Terms | Documents

Bank: Wizard Bank
Address: 4 The High Street, Anytown, Anyshire
Post Code: HS1 4GH
Telephone: 0111 234 7788
Facsimile: 0111 234 7789

Account Type: Bank Account
B/Soc Roll No.:
Account Name: A.R. McTernan
Account No.: 00045560
Sort Code: 11-22-33
IBAN:
BIC:
BACS Reference: 07755560

Second Account

Save   Close

Where an Account Number is less than eight digits, insert leading zeros, e.g. 00123456.

5 If you pay your employee by automatic credit transfer, enter the BACS Reference number

6 Click the Second Account button if you need to set up another bank account for this employee

7 When finished, click Save to record the details

You must complete all bank account details if you pay the employees by credit transfer.

Company/Employee Analysis

For businesses who wish to use departments, cost centres and employees for analysis purposes this can be achieved by appropriately setting up their individual Employee Record. To enter this information, follow the steps below:

Don't forget

Departments, Cost Centres and Employee Analysis first need setting up using the Analysis tab from Company Settings.

 Select the employee required, and from the Employee Record click the Analysis tab

 Under Company Analysis select the relevant Department and Cost Centre from the drop-down lists

Complete necessary details for Employee Analysis

Don't forget

There are three types of Employee Analysis and you can customise them to your own business needs. In this example, Union Member and Job Title have been set up.

70

Employee Record - Ref: 2 - Mr Andrew Robert McTernan

New   Starter Form   Personnel   First   Previous   Next   Last   Add Photo

Personal | Employment | Pensions | Absence | Cars/Fuel | Banking | Analysis | History | Terms | Documents

Company Analysis
Department   6 - Programmers   Employee Access Level   0
Cost Centre   ACC - Accounts

Employee Analysis
Union Member   Yes   Notes
Job Title   Departmental Manager
Analysis3

Electronic Documents
Payslip Comment
Send via email ☑   Date confirmed   / /
Send to   Password

Save   Close

 Enter any text you wish to appear on the payslip, here

If you send documents electronically to your employee tick the Send via email box and complete the remaining details as necessary

Click Save to record the new details or Close to return to the Payroll Desktop without saving

Hot tip

It is always useful to store a scanned photograph of your employee with their record card, especially in the case of larger businesses, for identification purposes.

Employee Payment History

To obtain a quick overview of your employees' payment history details, use the History tab from the Employee Record.

To view an employee's payment history, do the following:

1 Select the employee required, and from the Employee Record click on the History tab

2 The window shows each payment processed for your employee, including Total Gross Pay

The History tab does not display any brought forward values.

Employee Record - Ref: 20 - Miss. Joanne Lisle

New | Starter Form | Personnel | First | Previous | Next | Last | Add Photo

Personal | Employment | Pensions | Absence | Cars/Fuel | Banking | Analysis | History | Terms | Documents

Tax Week	Tax Month	Date Processed	Tax Code	Week1/Month1	NI Category	Total Gross Pay	Total Net Pay	Notes
6	2	17/05/2016	810L	No	B	600.00	504.38	
8	2	31/05/2016	810L	No	B	600.00	504.18	
10	3	14/06/2016	810L	No	B	600.00	504.18	
11	3	21/06/2016	810L	No	B	600.00	504.38	
13	3	05/07/2016	810L	No	B	600.00	504.18	
15	4	19/07/2016	810L	No	B	600.00	504.38	
17	4	02/08/2016	810L	No	B	600.00	504.18	
19	5	16/08/2016	810L	No	B	600.00	504.18	
21	5	30/08/2016	810L	No	B	620.00	519.20	
23	6	13/09/2016	810L	No	B	620.00	519.00	
25	6	27/09/2016	810L	No	B	620.00	519.20	
27	7	11/10/2016	810L	No	B	620.00	519.00	
29	7	25/10/2016	810L	No	B	620.00	519.00	
31	8	08/11/2016	810L	No	B	620.00	519.20	
33	8	22/11/2016	810L	No	B	620.00	519.00	

No processing until / /   15920.00   View P11

Save   Close

Only after processing your employee's payroll will their payment details begin to appear on the History tab.

3 Click View P11 button to see NI Contributions

4 Click Help for an explanation of terms

View P11

National Insurance | P.A.Y.E. [1] | P.A.Y.E. [2] | Weekly Averages

Week No	Earnings Up To LEL	Earnings LEL To PT	Earnings PT To UEL	Total Contribution	Employee Contribution
2	222	84	314	61.88	18.42
4	222	84	314	61.88	18.42
6	222	84	314	61.88	18.42
8	222	84	314	61.88	18.42
10	222	84	314	61.88	18.42
12	222	84	314	61.88	18.42
14	222	84	314	61.88	18.42
16	222	84	314	61.88	18.42
18	222	84	314	61.88	18.42
20	222	84	314	61.88	18.42
22	222	84	314	61.88	18.42
24	222	84	314	61.88	18.42
26	222	84	314	61.88	18.42
28	222	84	314	61.88	18.42

Close | Help

5 Use tabs to preview P.A.Y.E. (Pay As You Earn) and Weekly Averages data

You can view employee payment history details, but you cannot edit any of this information.

6 When finished, click Close to return

...cont'd

From the Payroll toolbar, Reports option, Employee section you can print a P11 Deduction Card (NIC Details) and a P11 Deduction Card (P.A.Y.E. Details) for various selected employees.

7 Details of the Gross Pay for Tax of an employee for each tax period as well as various To Date figures are displayed on the P.A.Y.E. [1] tab

Week No	Gross Pay for Tax This Period	Gross Pay for Tax To Date	Free Pay To Date	Additional Pay To Date [K]	Taxable Pay To Date
2	594.50	594.50	311.90	0.00	282.60
4	594.50	1189.00	623.80	0.00	565.20
6	594.50	1783.50	935.70	0.00	847.80
8	594.50	2378.00	1247.60	0.00	1130.40
10	594.50	2972.50	1559.50	0.00	1413.00
12	594.50	3567.00	1871.40	0.00	1695.60
14	594.50	4161.50	2183.30	0.00	1978.20
16	594.50	4756.00	2495.20	0.00	2260.80
18	594.50	5350.50	2807.10	0.00	2543.40
20	594.50	5945.00	3119.00	0.00	2826.00
22	594.50	6539.50	3430.90	0.00	3108.60
24	594.50	7134.00	3742.80	0.00	3391.20
26	594.50	7728.50	4054.70	0.00	3673.80
28	594.50	8323.00	4366.60	0.00	3956.40

View P11 — National Insurance | P.A.Y.E. [1] | P.A.Y.E. [2] | Weekly Averages — Close | Help

8 Tax information can be viewed on the P.A.Y.E. [2] tab

9 Click the Weekly Averages tab for 12 or 13 week averages

If your employee is on a Week 1 or Month 1 code then the Total Tax Due To Date figure in the P.A.Y.E. [2] tab represents the total from when the selected employee started working for you and does not include any cumulative values from previous employment.

View P11 — National Insurance | P.A.Y.E. [1] | P.A.Y.E. [2] | Weekly Averages

TW	Total Hours	Total Pay	Updated
23	20.0000	229.22	12/09/2016
24	20.0000	229.22	19/09/2016
25	20.0000	229.22	26/09/2016
26	20.0000	229.22	03/10/2016
27	20.0000	229.22	10/10/2016
28	20.0000	229.22	17/10/2016
29	20.0000	229.22	24/10/2016
30	20.0000	229.22	31/10/2016
31	20.0000	229.22	07/11/2016
32	20.0000	229.22	14/11/2016
33	20.0000	229.22	21/11/2016
34	20.0000	229.22	28/11/2016
35	0.0000	0.00	/ /

Average Type
12 Week ⦿   13 Week ○

Averages
Weekly Pay — 229.22
Weekly Hours — 20.0000
Daily Hours — 4.0000

Payments included in calculation
No. of Payments — 12
Total Payments — 2750.64

Print | Close | Help

10 Click Close to return to the History tab

6 Cars, Fuel and Class 1A NIC

Learn how to maintain company car details, record fuel used and set Class 1A NI Contributions.

Hot tip

Let the New Car Wizard guide you through the stages of setting up your new car records.

Don't forget

Class 1A NIC is paid one year in arrears and will appear on the Form P32 Employer's Payment Record in month 3 of the following year. For example, Class 1A NIC due for a car used in tax year April 2016 to March 2017 will show on the P32 in June 2017, i.e. month 3.

Hot tip

Refer to Payroll Help for more information about legislation governing Class 1A NIC for company cars and fuel.

Cars and Fuel Records

Current government legislation makes employers, not employees, liable for National Insurance contributions on the value of company cars and the fuel they use.

Employees need to be earning over a specific figure per annum (including expenses and any benefits) before the employer is liable for NIC payments on the value of the company car and fuel provided to them. NIC also becomes due if the employee becomes a director. This is what is referred to as Class 1A National Insurance contributions.

To calculate the amount of liability due scale rates are applied which refer to the age of the car, its original market value, its engine capacity, number of business miles, Carbon Dioxide (CO2) emissions, etc.

Details for each employee provided with a company car are recorded on the Cars/Fuel tab of the Employee Record. Once this information has been entered, Sage Payroll will then automatically calculate the Class 1A NIC liability using the current legislation rates. Not all of this information is used for calculations; some is purely for recording purposes.

Preparing to set up your new car records checklist

Before creating your new car records you will need:

- The car registration number
- Its make and model
- The engine capacity
- List price of the car
- Date the car was first registered
- Date the car was first used
- Type of fuel or power used (i.e. petrol, diesel, etc.)
- CO2 emissions (Note: All cars registered from 1 January 1998 are required by law to be supplied with details of their CO2 emissions. Cars registered after 1 November 2000 have the CO2 emissions figure recorded on the Vehicle Registration Certificate V5C.)

Creating New Car Records

Once you have followed the checklist on page 74 and have collated all your information together, you can now begin setting up your new car records using the New Car Wizard.

To set up your new car records

1 Select your Employee Record and click the Cars/Fuel tab

2 Click the New Car button to start the Wizard

3 Click Next

4 Enter the car details, using the drop-down list where available

5 Enter CO2 emissions then click Next

6 Complete the car valuation details in the next screen

7 Enter any sum payable by the employee for private use (per year)

8 Click Next

For most cars, the CO2 emissions are shown on the Vehicle Registration Certificate (V5C).

Select the No Approved CO2 Emissions check box if the car was registered before 1 January 1998, is a one off model or a privately imported car from outside the EC, and it does not have an approved CO2 emissions figure. The Standard Charge will then be calculated using the car's engine size.

75

Non-Standard Accessories refers to the value of any accessories added to the car after it was purchased. However, accessories of less than £100 are ignored.

...cont'd

Don't forget

A car is considered as classic if it is 15 years old or more, has a classic value of £15,000 or more and if the current market value is greater than the car's original market value. Also, Classic accessories are assumed to be part of the classic car price.

Don't forget

The Remove Car Wizard, activated by clicking the Remove Car button on the Cars/Fuel tab, will allow you to keep a car record without removing the mileage information, or will delete all of the details about the specified car.

9 Tick here if fuel is provided for the employee's private use

10 Click Next to continue

11 If applicable, enter when the employee stopped using the car

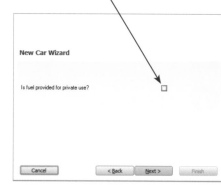

12 If you entered a tick in Step 9, enter the actual business mileage for the appropriate year

13 Click Next

14 On the next screen check that the new car information you have entered is all correct

15 If not, use the back button to return and make any amendments

16 If correct, click Finish to create the new car record and display the P46(Car) Details. Click OK when done

Removing Car Details

The occasion may arise when you need to remove mileage details, but retain the car record, or delete all details about a certain car. Sage Payroll lets you do both of these actions through the Remove Car Wizard.

Use the Enter Mileage button on the Cars/Fuel tab to quickly view the Employee Mileage Log.

To remove an employee's mileage details

1 Select your Employee Record and click the Cars/Fuel tab

2 Click the Remove Car button to start the Wizard, then Next

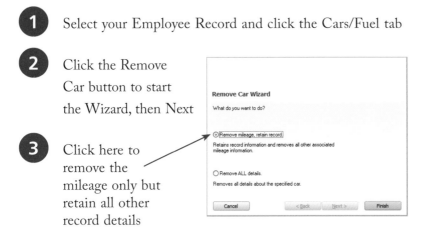

3 Click here to remove the mileage only but retain all other record details

4 Click Finish to complete the action and return to the Cars/Fuel tab

To delete all car details

1 Select your Employee Record and click the Cars/Fuel tab

2 Click the Remove Car button to start the Wizard, then Next

3 Click here if you want to remove all details about the specified car

When you remove the car mileage for a selected car, note that the Mileage Log details are also blanked.

4 Click Finish. Sage Payroll will prompt you if a P46(Car) certificate is required for a particular car

Entering Mileage Records

Having set up your employee car details, you now need to keep an accurate record of the business mileage covered. Sage Payroll will then use this information to calculate the Class 1A National Insurance Contributions.

Remember that mileage records will normally be recorded in the current tax year but the Class 1A NICs on company cars are calculated using the annual mileage for the previous tax year.

To enter mileage records, do the following:

 Select your employee's record and click the Cars/Fuel tab

 Click on the Enter Mileage button to bring up the Employee Mileage Log

 Enter the Journey Date and Journey Details

Don't forget

When you need reports containing information about car details, mileage and Class 1A NIC, these are available within the Reports, Cars & Fuel section.

Don't forget

You are required to keep accurate and up-to-date records of all business mileage details.

Employee Mileage Log ✕

Car Registration | WIZ 123 | Make and Model | Alfa Romeo Giulietta

Journey Date	Journey Details	Business Mileage
25/11/2016	Aberdeen and Return	446
29/11/2016	Bristol and Return	418
02/12/2016	Birmingham NEC and Return	184
/ /		

Total Mileage | 1048

OK | Close | Help

 Enter the Business Mileage

 The Total Mileage for all recorded journeys is calculated for you by Sage Payroll

 Click OK to save details when finished or Close to exit the Mileage Log without saving

Hot tip

Quickly view details of your liability by clicking the Class 1A NIC button on the Cars/Fuel tab.

Entering Class 1A NIC Details

Employers who provide a car to an employee for both private and business use as well as providing fuel for the vehicle are liable for payment of Class 1A NI contributions. However, the employee is not liable to make any of these payments.

These Class 1A NIC details are set up within the Employee Record as follows:

To enter your Class 1A NIC details

1 Select your employee's record and click the Cars/Fuel tab

2 Click on the Class 1A NIC button to bring up the NI Contributions details

3 Standard Charges display automatically once a mileage record has been created

4 Enter any Other Days Unavailable, if applicable

Class 1A National Insurance Contributions are due on most taxable benefits provided to employees and are paid by employers only. For more information about Class 1A NICs contact HMRC or visit the **www.hmrc.gov.uk** site.

The standard charge for fuel is based upon the engine capacity of the car and the type of fuel, i.e. diesel, petrol, etc.

Class 1A NIC   ✕

Car Registration   WIZ 123   Make and Model   Alfa Romeo Giulietta

NI Contribution

Charge Type	Standard Charges	Other Days Unavailable	Reimbursed by Employee	Revised Charges	Class 1A NIC
Cars	4500	0	0	4500	621.00
Fuel	5525	0	0	5525	762.45

Total   1383.45

Employer's Class 1A NIC Rate (%)   13.80

     OK   Close   Help

---

5 Enter any contributions paid by the employee for payment of fuel and/or use of the car, here

6 Note the Employer's Class 1A NIC percentage rate used

7 The Class 1A NIC is calculated using the Step 6 rate

If a car is unavailable to an employee for 30 days or more you need to enter the number of days within the Other Days Unavailable field. For example, cars off the road and in for repair after an accident.

...cont'd

Hot tip

Because Sage Payroll uses current legislation to calculate any Class 1A NICs due to HMRC, you must remember to ensure the software is up-to-date by checking for updates.

 Note the updated Revised Charges figures after applying any reimbursements or days unavailable

Class 1A NIC						×
Car Registration		WIZ 123	Make and Model		Alfa Romeo Giulietta	

NI Contribution

Charge Type	Standard Charges	Other Days Unavailable	Reimbursed by Employee	Revised Charges	Class 1A NIC
Cars	4500	31	0	4118	568.28
Fuel	5525	31	0	5057	697.87

Total 1266.15

Employer's Class 1A NIC Rate (%) 13.80

OK   Close   Help

 When all changes have been made, click the Close button to save the Class 1A NIC details entered

 If the employee has more than one car, click in the Car Registration field on the Cars/Fuel tab to bring up a list

11 Select another car and click OK

Don't forget

Click the P46(Car) button and make sure the correct boxes are ticked in the P46(Car) window whenever you set up a New Car.

Employee Record - Ref: 1 - Miss. Fiona McGarey

New   Starter Form   Personnel   First   Previous   Next   Last   Add Photo

Personal | Employment | Pensions | Absence | Cars/Fuel | Banking | Analysis | History | Terms | Documents

Car Registration	JB MICRO		Date First Registered	01/10/2016
Make and Model		Registration	Model	2016
Engine Capacity		JB MICRO	AUDI A6	
Classic Car Value		JB MICRO 2	VW Golf GTi	0
List Price Inc Std Accs				120
Non-Std Accessories				
Capital Contribution			OK Close	
Type of Fuel or Power	Petrol		Date Fuel Withdrawn	/ /
			Fuel Reinstated	

New Car   Remove Car   Enter Mileage   Class 1A NIC   P46 (Car)

Save   Close

 Repeat from Step 2 to make entries for the other car

7 Payments to Employees

See how to process different payment types and methods (e.g. monthly, weekly, cheque, cash, BACS etc.) and learn how to enter hours and rates of pay for your hourly paid staff. Sick pay, maternity pay, deductions, loans, attachments, manual pension payments, absence and advancing holiday pay are also covered.

When entering payments a warning message will appear if the payroll has already been updated for this period.

Don't forget

Parts 1 & 2 of the Payment Summary Report must be printed BEFORE updating the payroll, whilst part 3 needs printing AFTER the update.

Hot tip

Refer to Chapter 4, (page 46) for details of how to set up the Nominal Link.

Processing your Payroll

Once your employees' records and payment types have been set up you are ready to process your payroll and pay your employees.

You will have employees with different payment types; for example, some will require paying weekly, others fortnightly and some four-weekly or monthly. Different methods of payment can also be set for your employees and include cash payment, cheque, BACS and credit transfer.

Where employees are hourly-paid you can enter the number of hours they work, which will be multiplied against the rate to calculate the gross amount.

Whilst preparing your payroll, you will need to check if any sick pay, maternity pay or holiday pay needs including. Attachments and deductions may also be applied to some of your employees.

Once all the information has been processed, pre-update reports must be printed and checked for any discrepancies before the records are actually updated. This Payment Summary consists of three parts, namely: two pre-update and one post-update report.

Part 1: Gives a payroll summary for the period
         being processed

Part 2: Gives a National Insurance summary

Part 3: Gives a Year to Date summary

After the payroll has been processed, you may need to use the Nominal Link to update your Sage Accounts data. There may be leavers to deal with and P45s to produce. The P32 Employers Payment Record will need submitting to HMRC.

Initially, it is useful to follow the payroll checklist opposite to remind you of the different procedures that contribute to the processing of your payroll.

Payroll Processing Checklist

Before processing your payroll you might find it useful to work through the checklist below:

- Check that Government legislation has not changed. Check for updates if necessary.
- Create any new Employee Records.
- Note any changes to your employees' pay rates.
- Check all SSP details have been entered or are ready to enter.
- Have to hand details of any holiday payments to make.
- Ensure you have set up any court order details relating to an employee.
- Check the previous payroll date has been updated.
- Check or enter your payroll processing date.
- Reset Payments (where applicable).
- Enter your employee payments, deductions, attachments and loans.
- Print your pre-update Payment Summary report. Check and correct any mistakes, and reprint.
- Print payslips, cheques etc.
- Print all reports you may require.
- Make a pre-update backup copy to removable media.
- Update the records.
- Update your accounts program via the Nominal Link (optional).
- Deal with any leavers and produce their P45s.
- At the month end print the P32 report to show payments due to HMRC.

The Reset Payments Wizard (covered on pages 85-86) will only reset the 'Hours/ No' value for fixed payment types. Global payment types contain values applicable to all employees and cannot be reset.

Updating your records will also update all the P11 information.

Use Pre-update Reports... from the Payroll Tasks list, Summary section, to preview or print your Payment Summary (Parts 1 & 2).

Payroll Processing Date

It is important to check the processing date before you start to process your payroll. The date is normally the day you pay your employees, e.g. if you pay your employees on a monthly basis, the processing date may be the last working day of the month.

This date calculates the tax week or month and determines the amount of NI contributions and tax, etc. you deduct from your employees' pay.

To check or change the Process Date, do the following:

The payroll processing date is used to calculate the correct tax week or tax month.

1 From the toolbar click Tasks, Payroll then Change Process Date...

2 Check the Process Date. Use the Calendar button to change the Process Date if necessary

Always check you are using the correct Process Date. It can be entered when you start the Sage Payroll program.

3 Note that the Tax Period is changed automatically for you

4 Click OK to save changes or Cancel to abandon

If your Sage Payroll allows you to move between different companies, the program will prompt you to check the processing date.

Note: If you have changed the Process Date to a new date, to allow you to process your payroll in advance, for example, it is important to remember to change it back to the correct date before performing any other tasks.

Resetting Payments

Before entering new payments for the current payroll period, it may be necessary to clear certain payment details from your employees' records for the last period.

An example of this is where the number of overtime hours varies from week to week. However, the rest of the payroll details can remain the same. To reset your employees' payments do as follows:

1 From the Payroll Tasks list select Reset Payments...

2 The Reset Payments Wizard Welcome screen appears to inform you what the Wizard will help you do

3 After reading the notes, click Next to continue through the Wizard

4 Deselect any employees from this list whose payments do not need changing

5 Select whether to Selectively Reset each payment in turn or to Clear All payments in one go, then click Next

Global Payments contain values which apply to all employees so you cannot use the Reset Payments Wizard to change them.

The Reset Payments Wizard is also available from the Sage Payroll toolbar using the Wizards option.

85

If you make a mistake simply click Cancel to abandon your changes and exit the Reset Payments Wizard.

...cont'd

Hot tip

From this screen you can reset all values for all payments OR check through each individual payment. From the drop-down lists you can then decide whether you wish to Retain, Clear or use Default settings.

Hot tip

Use the vertical scroll bar if you need to view all your payment types.

 6 Set Hours, Rates and Multipliers (for all payments) as appropriate here

7 For individual payments, choose an option from the drop-down list

Reset Payments Wizard

Select whether you want to retain, clear or set to the default value from the employee record for all payments. If you would prefer to reset each payment individually use the table below.

Hours Default   Multiplier Retain   Rates Retain

Description	Hours/No	Multiplier	Rate
Salary	Default	N/A	Retain
Commission	Default	N/A	Default
Expenses	Retain	N/A	Retain
	Clear		
	Default		

Cancel   < Back   Next >   Finish

8 Click Next

9 ALL deductions can be reset here

Reset Payments Wizard

Select the appropriate button to reset the values for all deductions. Alternatively work through the list of values below, choosing which deductions to retain, clear or set to default.

Hours Default   Rates Default

Description	Hours/No	Rate
Professional Subscription	Default	Retain
Union	Default	Default
	Retain	
	Clear	
	Default	

Cancel   < Back   Next >   Finish

10 Use the drop-down list to reset individual deductions here

11 Click Next

12 Retain or Clear any Statutory Payments in this screen as necessary

Reset Payments Wizard

Select the values you want to reset from the list below.

Description	Action
Attachments	Retain
Statutory Sick Pay	Retain
	Clear
	Retain
Statutory Maternity Pay	Retain
Statutory Paternity Pay	Retain
Statutory Adoption Pay	Retain
Shared Parental Pay	Retain

Cancel   < Back   Next >   Finish

13 Click Next

14 Click Finish to save changes and return to the Payroll Desktop

Reset Payments Wizard

You have completed the Reset Payments Wizard.

Click Back to change any of the details entered on a previous page, or click Finish to reset the selected payments and complete the Reset Payments Wizard.

Cancel   < Back   Next >   Finish

Processing your Payments

Payment information is entered using the Enter Payments option from the Payroll menu. This payroll information is then used for automatically generating your employees' net pay. To process your payments do as follows:

1 From the Employee list box, first select all the employees you wish to pay and process

2 From the toolbar click Tasks, Payroll then Enter Payments...

3 For the first employee, if a default number of hours has not yet been set up, enter this employee's hours in the Hours/No field

4 If a rate needs updating, do so now

5 Tick if it is the final payment because an employee is leaving

6 Click Save/Next to move to the next record

7 A message informs you if a Tax Refund is due, as in this example. Click OK

The Tax field displays whether the payment is pre-tax or post-tax.

Use the Select button to bring up an employee list from which you can quickly choose the employee to enter payment information for.

Select

Before leaving a record, it is best to check other details, e.g. SSP/SMP.

Processing your Deductions

To process deductions for your employees, the information needs to be entered using the Deductions tab from the Enter Payments window. Commonly used deductions include union fees/professional fees, health schemes, recreation activities, etc. Chapter 12 shows you how to set up deductions for both your company and your employees. To process your deductions, follow the steps below:

 From the Enter Payments window, click the Deductions tab

 Deduction types assigned to this employee are displayed

 Enter the number of deductions for a payment in the Hours/No field (usually 1)

 Enter the appropriate deduction rate for the deduction type in the Rate field

Don't forget

If a default number has already been set up for the deduction type in the Hours/No field, it will appear automatically.

Beware

You cannot change the default rate for global or fixed deduction types.

Hot tip

Use the Add Deduction button to quickly add a new deduction to the employee's record.

 Carefully check that all deductions are recorded accurately

 Click Save/Next to move to the next record, or click Close to abandon and return to the Sage Payroll Desktop

Processing Attachments

Sage Payroll will process these attachments of earnings automatically for those employees liable for these deductions. To process these attachments, follow the steps below:

1 From the Enter Payments window, click the Attachments tab

2 Attachment types assigned to this employee are displayed

3 The Attach Value field shows the amount being deducted

4 The Attach Earnings field shows the earnings from which the attachment is deducted

The Amount Deducted field shows the actual deduction after taking into account any protected earnings.

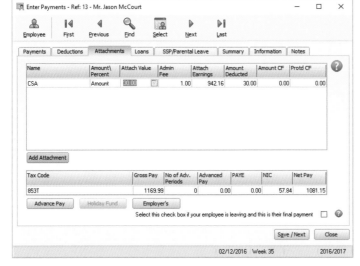

If the whole amount is unable to be processed for this period, the Amount CF field shows the value carried forward to the next period. The Protd CF field shows any protected earnings which are also carried forward.

5 Use the Add Attachment button to create a new attachment if required

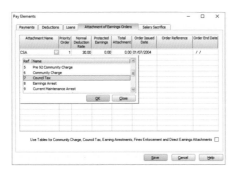

6 Click Save/Next to move to the next record

See pages 149-152 for more information on setting up and processing attachments.

Hot tip

You can also use the Recording SSP or ShPP buttons to quickly record SSP and Parental Leave details and information.

Don't forget

If you are recording shared parental leave absence from the Enter Payments window, you must first have set up appropriate shared parental leave details for that employee.

SSP and Parental Leave

When an employee is absent from work you can record details of their absence via their Employee Record, as shown in Chapter 6. For example, the type of absence, such as holidays or sick leave, and the relevant dates. You can then use the diary to see when and why an employee is absent.

However, you can also quickly record an employee's sickness or shared parental leave details when you pay them, using the Enter Payments option as follows:

 Select the required employee, click Enter Payments... then select the SSP/Parental Leave tab

 Select the first date of absence, hold down the left mouse button and drag to the last absence date

 Right-click the selected range and choose the absence type you want to record

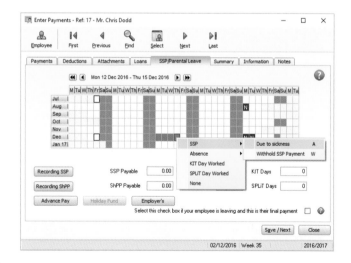

 Check details in the Absence Information window and add a comment if required

 Click OK to update the diary

Processing Loans

Sage Payroll includes the facility to process loans. If an employee is repaying a loan, once set up, any repayments can be taken directly from their salary. To process a loan, follow the steps below:

1 From the Enter Payments window, click the Loans tab

2 Loans assigned to this employee are displayed

3 The Repayment Due field shows the amount being deducted and can be increased or decreased if necessary

4 The Balance Carried Forward field shows the amount of loan still outstanding

Refer to Chapter 12 for more information about setting up and allocating new loans.

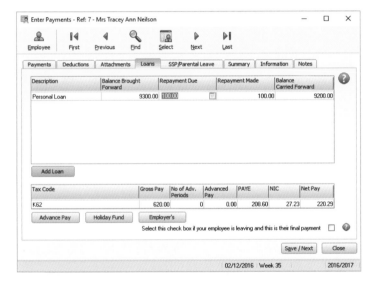

If your Company provides employee loans, use the Loans option to automatically deduct repayments from your employee's pay.

5 Use the Add Loan button to add or create a new loan if required

6 Click Save/Next to move to the next record

When a loan is almost paid, Sage Payroll automatically adjusts the end repayment so that the loan is not overpaid.

Hot tip

Refer to Chapter 10 for details on processing SMP payments.

Don't forget

EWC is the term describing the expected week of confinement, which always begins on a Sunday.

Don't forget

MPP stands for Maternity Pay Period. Refer to the Sage Payroll Help facility for more information.

Statutory Maternity Pay

Statutory Maternity Pay (SMP) is a legal requirement from HMRC and entitles employees who stop work to have a baby to a certain amount of pay during their time off work, provided they meet the qualifying conditions. As Sage Payroll will calculate the correct figures for anyone eligible for SMP, the appropriate information, dates, etc. needs entering as follows:

1 Open the record for the employee you require

2 Select the Absence tab

3 Click on the SMP button

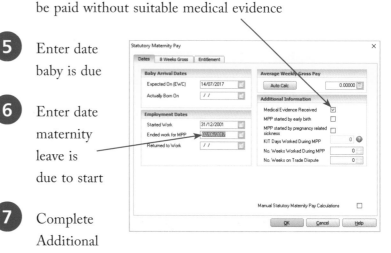

4 In the Dates tab, tick here to show receipt of medical evidence confirming when the baby is due. SMP cannot be paid without suitable medical evidence

5 Enter date baby is due

6 Enter date maternity leave is due to start

7 Complete Additional information as necessary

8 At a later date, if the employee has worked during MPP enter the number of full or part weeks in the No. Weeks Worked During MPP field

9 Click here to calculate Average Weekly Gross Pay OR enter a value

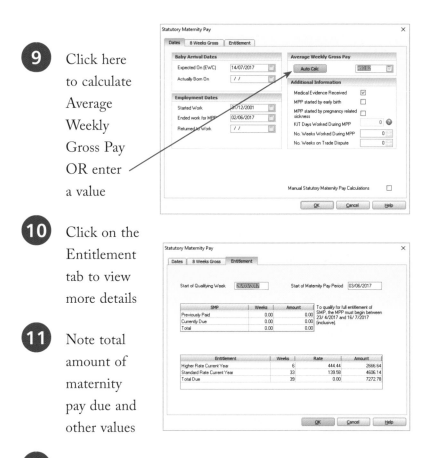

If your employee works during MPP, they lose entitlement to SMP for the weeks worked.

10 Click on the Entitlement tab to view more details

11 Note total amount of maternity pay due and other values

Actually Born On field for baby's date of birth and mother's Returned to Work details can only be completed once the event has happened.

12 For more SMP information, click the middle tab to view 8 Weeks Gross Payment History, 8 Weeks Average Earnings and Payments Used in Calculations details. If Sage Payroll has been used to pay the employee during the eight week period prior to the qualifying week, the table shows details of the payments made in each period

If you have not selected the Manual Statutory Maternity Pay Calculations check box, you need to manually enter SMP payments for your employees when processing your payroll. For example, when you start using the Payroll program part way through the tax year.

13 Check or note all values. If there is no payment history during this period, simply enter an average for the eight weeks in the Gross Pay box

14 When done, click OK to save any changes, else click Close to exit

Viewing Payment Summary

Sage Payroll lets you view both your payments and deductions for a selected employee together. This is available using the Summary tab from the Enter Payments window as follows:

 Select the desired employee or employees then click Enter Payments... from the Tasks list

 Click on the Summary tab

 Current Payments and Deductions are displayed

 Click here to view Employer's NI and Pension contributions

 Click OK to return to the Summary tab

Regularly use the Summary tab to quickly check that any additional payments or deductions you make have been correctly recorded.

To view an itemised breakdown for an employee's Income Tax, National Insurance, Statutory Payments, Pension, Student Loans, Attachments, Holiday Fund, Loans and Salary Sacrifice, select the Information tab

Click on each group in turn to view details

 Click Save/Next to move to the next record or Close to exit

Manual Pension Payments

Manual pension contributions need processing as part of your normal processing routine. The Pension Scheme will need setting up first and named, for example, Manual Entry, then the scheme will need applying to the relevant employee.

Each time the payroll is updated, the Pension's YTD figures will accumulate. To enter an employee's pension, manually select the desired employee or employees then do the following:

1 Click Enter Payments... from the Tasks list and select the Summary tab

2 A zero value means no contributions have yet been made

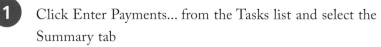

3 Click here to enter Pension Contributions

4 Enter your employee's pension details here for the current processing period

5 In the next field, enter any holiday pension contributions if you are paying your employee any holiday pay during this processing period

6 Click OK to save or Cancel to abandon and return to the Summary tab

Before entering your pension payments manually, you must have set up a pension scheme which is Fixed, with no default amount or percentage entered. Do this by selecting Pension Schemes... from the Company Tasks list.

You cannot enter Additional Voluntary Contributions (AVCs) when processing pensions manually.

Advancing Holiday Pay

Hot tip

When you advance an employee's holiday pay, Sage Payroll will automatically flag them as being on holiday. This then prevents them being accidentally processed again during the holiday period.

Don't forget

When entering a value for Periods to Advance, weekly paid staff need the number of whole weeks they will be on holiday for and monthly paid staff need a whole month period entering. Single days are not valid.

To record an employee's holiday pay in advance, use the Advance Pay button from the Enter Payments window. This method ensures your employee's tax is calculated correctly over the whole holiday period instead of on a lump sum payment. To do this, follow the steps below:

1 Click on the Advance Pay button at the foot of the Enter Payments window for your selected employee

2 Enter the number of payment periods you wish to advance, e.g. 1

3 Enter relevant payment information here

4 Remember to also enter any Deductions, Attachments or Loans

5 Click OK to save

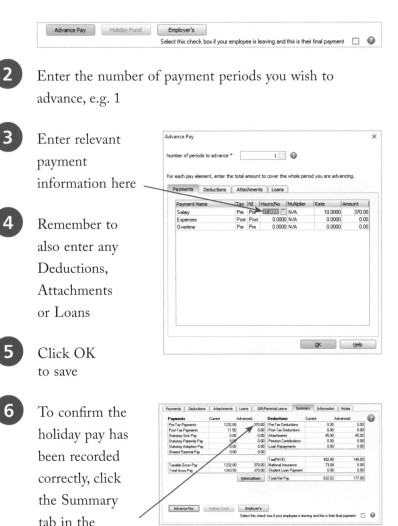

6 To confirm the holiday pay has been recorded correctly, click the Summary tab in the Enter Payments window and check the Payments, Advanced column

8 Processing Procedures

Produce your pre-update reports so you can check payment details before updating the payroll. Take backups, correct errors, process leavers, restart an employee or make a director.

Printing Pre-update Reports

Once processing is complete you must produce your pre-update reports. Several pre-update reports are available for you to use after entering the payment details; for example, Payment Summary, Attachment of Earnings Summary and Update Records Check Report. These reports will help you check payment details before updating the payroll.

To run payroll reports

Within Pre-update Reports, the reports are grouped into sections: Payslips, Cheques, BACS, Analysis, Summary and User Defined.

 1 From the Employee List, select all the employees required for pre-update reports

Use the Print button if you are certain there is no need to preview a report first.

98

2 Click Pre-update Reports... from the Payroll Tasks list

3 Click OK or as appropriate to any information messages

4 Select the type of report you require here

If you use Microsoft Outlook, a report may be sent as an attachment using the Email button on the menu bar.

5 The list view contains a variety of reports

6 From the list of reports and layouts, select the one needed

7 From the
Reports
toolbar,
click Preview

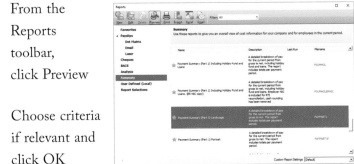

8 Choose criteria
if relevant and
click OK

9 A preview of the report is generated for you to check

10 For a hard copy, click Print at the top of the preview

A report can be saved
as a file (e.g. Excel, PDF,
etc.) for preview later or
for use in a presentation.

Always check the
Payment Summary
carefully for discrepancies
before updating your
records, to avoid having
to make corrections later.

11 Click OK from
the dialog box
unless you
need to change
printer, in which
case first select
a printer from the
drop-down list

Having printed your pre-
update reports, you need
to make a pre-update
backup. See page 100.

Updating your Records

After printing pre-update reports and making a pre-update backup it is time to update the employees' payment records. The Update Records Wizard will update the cumulative totals, add the current processing period to the P11 deduction cards and maintain historical information. The wizard even prompts you to make a backup in case you've forgotten.

To make a backup

Make a backup whilst using the Update Records Wizard.

1 With the employees you wish to process selected, from the Payroll Tasks list click Update Records...

2 Click Yes to close any reminders and continue

Sage backs up all data files into one file. The filename contains the company name followed by the tax week, the tax year and a file extension, e.g. SagePay. companyname.4316.001 = Tax Week 43, Tax Year 2016/2017.

3 On the Update Records Wizard Welcome screen click the Backup... button

4 The next window shows any previous backups and the path where they are stored. This is the path used when you took your first backup and where subsequent ones were saved

After updating your records, you must make a post-update backup.

5 Click Next to continue through the Backup Wizard

100

6 Select the files to be included in the backup. Data Files is selected for you by default

Backup Wizard
This page enables you to specify which files will be included in the Backup procedure.

Default Files
Data Files
RTI Files
Pension Data Files
Picture Files
Report Files
Template Files
Document Files

☑ Use this data as the 'Last Known Good' data.

Cancel   < Back   Next >   Finish

7 Click Next to continue

Clearly label your security backup media to avoid corrupting or deleting important information.

8 If you want to use a different path or filename for your backup, enter it now. Use the Browse button to help you

Backup Wizard
This page allows you to accept or change the path and/or the file name of your backup.
Type in the field below, or use the Browse button to enter a path and filename.
Example file name shown below.
SagePay.CoName.4609.001 - Sage Pay . Company Name . Week Number Current Year
Path
C:\Users\Bill\Documents\SagePay.Wizard Training Limited.3516.001   Browse

Cancel   < Back   Next >   Finish

If records have already been updated and they contain errors, often the only way to remove incorrect details is to restore a backup of the data files.

9 Click Next to continue

10 Click Finish to create the backup. Remember to clearly label your backup media as appropriate

Backup Wizard
The Backup will begin when you click the Finish button.
You may click the Back button if you want to change the details on previous pages.

Cancel   < Back   Next >   Finish

11 The Backup Status is displayed to show how it is progressing

Backup Status
Disk No   1
File Name   PAYROLL.MDB
File Size   43487232   bytes
Progress
    Cancel

If a backup is restored, all payroll frequency types that have been run since the last backup was taken will need to be run again.

12 When the backup has finished, click OK to close

Sage Payroll   ×
ⓘ The backup has been successful.
    OK

...cont'd

Updating your records

Don't forget

Check that all processing details in the Update Records Wizard are correct before continuing with the update. For example, all employees have been updated for the previous period.

Hot tip

The Previous column quickly shows whether or not an Employee Record was updated for the tax period immediately before this one.

Hot tip

Let the Nominal Link Wizard guide you through posting your payroll payments directly to your accounts program. See page 103.

 1 The Update Records Wizard appears, displaying information about employees to be updated

2 Click Next to continue if all details are correct

3 Employees' payroll is now calculated. Depending on the speed of your computer you may see the recalculating window

4 A list of employees' records to be processed and updated is displayed. Deselect records not required

5 Click Finish to update the records

 6 Click OK to close the update complete box and return to the Payroll Desktop

Posting Nominal Link Payments

Once you have updated your payroll, use the Nominal Link Wizard to process your payroll postings to your accounts data. Also see page 51.

Use of the Nominal Link is only possible if it has first been set up, as shown on page 46. It transfers your payroll information into your accounts program so you don't have to do it manually. Do the following to post your payroll data after updating records:

1 Go into your accounts program, i.e. Sage 50 Accounts, and make a backup of your company accounts data. This is because posting nominal link payments is not reversible so if you make a mistake you can restore your accounts data and run the posting again

2 From the Employee List area on the Sage Payroll Desktop, select the payment period type, e.g. Monthly. Remember that you can only process one type at a time

3 The employee details list changes to show only the employees for the chosen payment period type

Beware

Your nominal link settings must be configured before using the Nominal Link.

Don't forget

The Nominal Link can only post one payment type at a time, i.e. Monthly, Weekly, etc.

![Sage 50 Payroll V22 screenshot showing the Employee List with employees including McGarey Fiona, Bradley Derek, Watts Neilson, Harvison Richard, Kerr Richard, Willis Richard, and the Payroll Tasks list with Nominal Link highlighted]

4 Click Nominal Link... from the Payroll Tasks list

Don't forget

Remember that the Nominal Link can only be posted after the payroll has been updated.

...cont'd

Beware

Ensure you have made at least one backup copy of your accounts data before using the Nominal Link Wizard.

Don't forget

If you have difficulty setting up the Nominal Link, always check that you have configured the appropriate nominal codes in the P&L or BS Analysis tab of the Nominal Link Settings window (see page 47).

Don't forget

You will only be given the option of choosing a company if you are using Sage 50 Accounts multi-company version and have more than one company set up.

5 The Nominal Link Wizard appears ready to guide you through the stages of posting your payments to your accounts data

6 Click Next to continue through the posting stages

Nominal Link Wizard

Welcome to the Nominal Link Wizard.

This wizard helps you to complete your nominal link postings.

IMPORTANT: You must take a backup of your accounts data files before you continue.

Cancel   < Back   Next >   Finish

7 Select the process date you want to use as a starting point for your nominal link postings, and Click Next

Nominal Link Wizard

Which payroll processing date do you want to use as a starting point for your nominal link postings ?

Process Date	Week	Month
21/10/2016	29	7
28/10/2016	30	7
04/11/2016	31	7
11/11/2016	32	8
18/11/2016	33	8
25/11/2016	34	8
02/12/2016	35	8
09/12/2016	36	9

Cancel   < Back   Next >   Finish

8 Check the correct employees are shown in the next window. If not, click Cancel or Back should you need to make changes, else click Next

Nominal Link Wizard

The following employees will be included in the nominal link procedure.

Ref	Surname	Forename
1	McGarey	Fiona
5	Bradley	Derek
11	Watts	Neilson
12	Harvison	Richard
14	Kerr	Richard
24	Willis	Richard

Cancel   < Back   Next >   Finish

9 Enter a Transaction Reference and check details in the window showing which options will be used for your postings

Nominal Link Wizard

The following options will be used for your postings.

Posting Destination	Instant Accounts / Sage 50 Accou
Transaction Reference	MONTH08
Transaction Date	02/12/2016
Group Transactions	☑

Cancel   < Back   Next >   Finish

10 If not required, untick Group Transactions then click Next

11 Click Print for a paper copy of the postings in case you need to check anything later

Nominal Link Wizard

The following transactions will be posted to Instant Accounts / Sage 50 Accounts.

Narrative	Journal	Amount	Nominal Code	Cost Centre	Dept.
Net Wages	Cr	10562.59	2220		
National Insurance	Cr	1498.13	2211		
PAYE	Cr	2462.82	2210		
Deductions	Cr	254.56	7000		
Payments	Dr	13872.25	7000		
Employers NIC	Dr	1102.35	7006		

Click 'Finish' to post the Transactions.   [Print]   [Send To Excel]

[Cancel]   [< Back]   [Next >]   [Finish]

12 Click Finish to post the Bank Payments

Hot tip

It is advisable to print a list of payroll transactions for checking purposes before updating your accounts package.

13 The Nominal Link Wizard prepares the transactions for posting and checks access to Sage Accounts. The Logon window appears when the link has been established

Nominal Link Wizard

Please wait while the Nominal Link Wizard posts the transactions.

Task Progress   [▭▭▭▭▭▭▭]

[Cancel]   [< Back]   [Next >]   [Finish]

Logon   ×

Sage Data Objects   [OK]
Please enter your logon name and   [Cancel]
Logon Name: [   ]
Password: [   ]

14 Enter the logon details for your Sage Accounts and click OK to post Nominal Transactions

15 When the Nominal Link Wizard has finished posting your transactions, details of postings are shown and a confirmation appears

Nominal Link Wizard

Please wait while the Nominal Link Wizard posts the transactions.

Task Progress   [   ]

6 Transaction(s) Posted
0 Transaction(s) Unposted

[Cancel]   [< Back]   [Next >]   [Finish]

Don't forget

If there are discrepancies in the posting information, a posting will be made to the Mispostings nominal account (9999).

16 Click OK to close the Nominal Link Wizard

Sage Payroll   ×

ⓘ Nominal Link has finished posting your transactions.

[OK]

Processing Leavers

Employees who have left the company can be marked as leavers after their final payroll payment has been updated. Their Employee Record will remain on the system until all the Year End procedures have been completed, unless they have a company car.

For leavers with company cars, their details must be retained on the payroll for an additional tax year. This information will be required for Class 1A NIC calculations as explained in Chapter 6. To mark an employee as a leaver, do the following:

Don't forget

Before marking an employee as a leaver they must have been included in their final payroll run.

 1 From the Payroll Desktop, select and open the Employee Record for the employee you wish to mark as a leaver

2 Click on the Employment tab

Hot tip

Use the Leaver Wizard to produce an employee's P45 and P11 forms.

106

3 Click the Leaver button to start the Leaver Wizard

4 Note the information on the Welcome screen and click Next

5 Check the details and amend the Leaving Date as necessary

Don't forget

Where an employee's status is changed to Director, the leaving date entered should be the final payroll run date as a non-Director.

6 You are now ready to print all the necessary leaver documentation, such as P45, P11 (NIC Details) and P11 (PAYE Details)

7 Use the drop-down list to select your first document

8 Click Print if you have put the correct stationery in the printer and are ready to print, else click Preview if you first need to check the details

9 When using pre-printed stationery, you may need to alter printer settings to align the printing

10 Repeat Steps 7-8 to print all required documents

11 Click Finish to change the employee's status to 'Leaver'

12 After the Leaver Wizard closes, note that the Leave Date has been entered for you on the Employee Record here

Save time and avoid wasting paper by always checking that you have put the correct stationery in your printer before sending any documents to print.

When processing a leaver it is always advisable to ensure that their status has been changed after running the Leaver Wizard. Simply check that the Leave Date has been entered for you on the Employee Record.

107

P32 Employers Summary Report

When the payroll processing has been completed and the payslips and P45s have been distributed, the P32 Employers Summary report must be printed.

To print the P32 Employers Summary Report:

 From the Sage Payroll toolbar, click Reports to bring up the Reports window

 Click on the Period End reports folder

 From the reports list, click on the Form P32 Employer's Payment Record report

 Click on the Print button on the toolbar

 Enter the Tax Month range in the criteria box

 Click OK to continue

 Click OK to print out the P32 report

Changing Payment Frequency

If you wish to change the frequency of an employee's pay, for example, monthly instead of weekly, simply do the following:

1 Make sure you have posted all outstanding payment transactions for the employee you are about to change

2 From the Payroll Desktop, select and open the Employee Record for the employee you wish to change the payment frequency for

3 Click the Employment tab

4 Click here for a list of available Payment Frequencies

When you mark an employee as a leaver and recreate their details, this means the employee will have two records. At the Year End only one P14 per employee can be submitted so the second P14 must be used, which records the cumulative values carried forward.

Employee Record - Ref: 2 - Mr Andrew Robert McTernan

New | Starter Form | Personnel | First | Previous | Next | Last | Add Photo

Personal | **Employment** | Pensions | Absence | Cars/Fuel | Banking | Analysis | History | Terms | Documents

Job Title	Data Entry Operator
Tax Code *	749L
NI Category *	A
N.I. Number *	JE 875764 C
Starter Form	
Start Date *	02/02/2009
Leave Date	/ /
Status	OK
RTI Payroll ID	c7773b5f43114c8f88f167829fae5715e

Operate net of foreign tax credit relief ☑

Week 1/Month 1 Basis ☐
Manual NI Entry ☐

Welfare To Work ☐
FPS Starter ☐
Non-UK Worker ☐

Works Number	2
Director Status	Non-Director
Payment Method	BACS
Payment Frequency	Weekly
Employment Type	Fortnightly / Four Weekly / Monthly / Weekly
Student Loan Start	25/04/2011
Student Loan Type	Plan Type 1
Student Loan End	/ /
Student Loan Priority	0
Protected Earnings	0.00

Pay Elements | Salary | YTD Values | Leaver | Apprentice

Save | Close

5 Select a new frequency

6 Click Yes to confirm

7 Click Save

Sage Payroll

❓ Are you sure you wish to change this employee's Pay Frequency ?

Yes | No

You should not change employee pay frequency until the end of the original pay frequency.

Changing to Director Status

Sage Payroll lets you change an employee's status to Director at any time during the tax year. Simply do the following:

From the Payroll Desktop, select and open the Employee Record for the employee you wish to change to Director status

Click the Employment tab

3 Click here for a Director Status list

Don't forget

Where an employee is flagged as a Director their NIC is automatically calculated on a yearly, cumulative basis, and not on a weekly or monthly basis as it is with your other employees.

Don't forget

Directors can elect to pay NIC period to period, the same as other employees. To do this, choose Director (Table Method) for Director Status. At the Year End, or if the Director leaves part-way through a tax year, the NI contributions must be recalculated on a year to date basis. Sage Payroll automatically calculates this for you at the year end, or when you set the Final Pay Run flag for a director who is leaving your company part-way through a tax year.

4 Select the relevant Director Status

5 Note the Date Directorship Began prompt

6 Click OK

7 Click Save to confirm

Sage Payroll ✕

ⓘ Changing the employee status to a 'Director' invokes special NI rules. We have set the 'Date Directorship Began' to the current processing date. If this is incorrect please amend it in the YTD Values - Director's NIC tab.

For further details please consult the on-line help or manual.

OK

To change the date directorship began

The date that the directorship started is automatically entered for you and is set to the current processing date. If the date the actual directorship began is different, change it on the Director's NIC tab:

1 On the Employee Record click the YTD Values button

Refer to Sage Help for additional information about Directors.

2 Select the Director's NIC tab

3 Enter the correct Date Directorship Began here

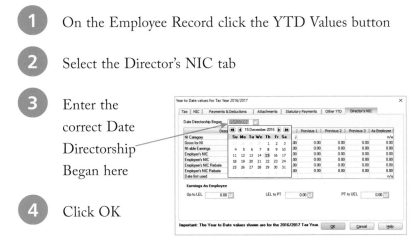

4 Click OK

Where employees leave your company and return within the same tax year, they must be added to the payroll as a new employee. You cannot reactivate their old Employee Record.

To place employees on hold

You can place employees on hold; for example, when someone is employed on a casual basis but currently not working for you. To temporarily exclude them from the processing routine, simply place them on hold, then take them off hold when they start paid work.

1 Open the Employee Record and select the Employment tab

2 Click in the Status field to bring up a drop-down box

Simply select OK in the Status field on the Employee Record to include your employee in the payroll processing routine again.

3 Select On Hold and click Save

Correcting Errors with Rollback

Sage Payroll lets you correct processing errors for one or more employees. The employee's basic record and car mileage details will not be affected, but all histories, absence records (SSP, SMP and holiday), cumulative values and update records will be amended. Use the Roll Back Employee Wizard as follows:

Beware

The Roll Back Employee Wizard is irreversible so always take a backup before you use it.

1 Click Rollback... from the Tasks menu

2 Click the Backup... button to ensure you back up the data first

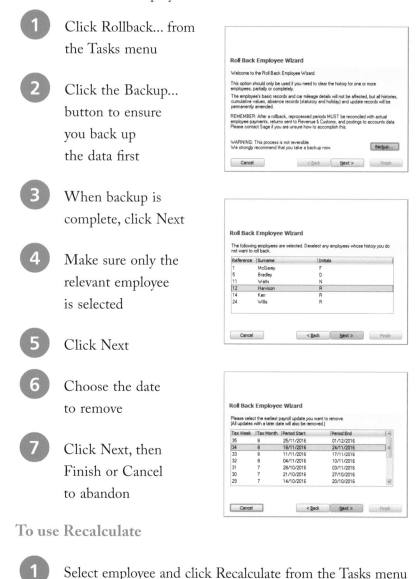

3 When backup is complete, click Next

Don't forget

After a rollback, reprocessed periods MUST be reconciled with actual employee payments, returns sent to HMRC and postings made to your Sage Accounts.

4 Make sure only the relevant employee is selected

5 Click Next

6 Choose the date to remove

7 Click Next, then Finish or Cancel to abandon

To use Recalculate

Beware

If you have no employees selected before running the Recalculate facility, then ALL employees will be recalculated.

1 Select employee and click Recalculate from the Tasks menu

2 Click Yes to confirm

9 Statutory Sick Pay

This chapter shows you how to set up and maintain your employees' Statutory Sick Pay. You will learn how to enter an employee's SSP details, with tips to help solve potential problems.

Hot tip

You need to be familiar with the following SSP terms:

PIW = Period of Incapacity for Work of four or more continuous calendar days (PIWs can be linked)

QD = Qualifying Day

WD = Waiting Day

Don't forget

A linked PIW is eight weeks or 56 days.

Don't forget

If a period of sickness is linked, the employee must be absent for no less than four consecutive days to receive SSP for the waiting days.

Introduction to SSP

From 6 April 1986 employers have been responsible for paying Statutory Sick Pay (SSP) to employees who are ill for a period of up to 28 weeks.

To be eligible for SSP the employee's average weekly earnings must be above the lower earnings limit for National Insurance Contributions (NICs). The average weekly earnings are calculated from the previous eight weeks' pay.

SSP qualifying conditions

The majority of employees are eligible for SSP providing they meet the following criteria:

- An employee must be over 16 years of age.
- The employee must be sick and absent from work for a minimum of four consecutive days (this includes holidays, weekends and any other day which the employee is not normally expected to work).
- SSP is not payable for the first three qualifying days of the period of sickness. These days are known as Waiting Days.
- The employee's Average Weekly Earnings (AWE) in the relevant period must be at or above the current National Insurance Lower Earnings Limit (LEL). For the 2016/2017 tax year, this is £112.00.
- You can't count a day as a sick day if an employee has worked for a minute or more before they go home sick.
- If an employee works a shift that ends the day after it started and becomes sick during the shift or after it has finished, the second day will count as a sick day.
- Where an employee has two PIWs with 56 or less days between the end of the first PIW and the start of the second PIW, the two PIWs are said to be linked and count as one continuous PIW. The employee then does not need any further Waiting Days before SSP starts.
- Employees are entitled to a maximum of 28 weeks SSP each time they begin a new PIW that does not link with a previous PIW.

SSP Checklist

Employers have certain responsibilities. These include establishing if an employee is eligible for SSP, that the correct SSP is paid for up to a maximum of 28 weeks and that appropriate tax and NI deductions are paid. HMRC requires that the following SSP records be kept:

For employers who operate SSP, records must include:

● Dates of sickness lasting at least four days, but you don't need to keep records of SSP paid. You can choose your recording method and HMRC may need to see these records if there's a dispute over payment of SSP.

Generally, you should ensure you itemise the following:

● First and last day that SSP liability arises.
● Number of weeks and days of SSP entitlement.
● Number of SSP qualifying days.

Sage Payroll processes and keeps a record of all SSP entitlements for your employees, but first, work through the checklist below:

● Are Qualifying Day Patterns set up?
● Has the employee been absent for four or more days in a row?
● Has a notice of sickness been received?
● Is the employee eligible for SSP?
● Are the absence days qualifying days?
● Check the employee's last eight weeks' average earnings. They must not be less than the lower earnings limit for NI to qualify for SSP.
● Check whether the employee has had an earlier period of absence within the last eight weeks. If so, the two PIWs may link.
● Decide which are the qualifying days for SSP.
● Process the SSP at the same time as you process an employee's normal earnings.

Refer to Sage Payroll Help for more information about linking PIWs.

Agency Workers/Contract Workers who are normally treated as employees for National Insurance Contributions purposes are also treated as employees for SSP purposes.

When unsure about an employee's SSP entitlement, contact HMRC for advice.

SSP Qualifying Days

Qualifying days are days agreed between the employer and employee. These days are normally when the employee is contractually required to be available for work; for example, Monday to Friday.

Once the days are agreed, a qualifying pattern needs allocating to each employee identifying the qualifying days for SSP entitlement. To set up your qualifying days, do the following:

Qualifying days need setting up BEFORE you process SSP.

1 From the Employee Record, click the Absence tab

2 Click the S.S.P. button

3 Click the Qualifying Days tab

4 Click here, select a qualifying days pattern and click OK to accept

5 Enter the qualifying pattern start date. This must be a SUNDAY

SSP qualifying patterns are set up from the Absence tab in the Company Settings.

6 Click OK to save or Close to exit

7 Click Yes to confirm changes or No to return to the Qualifying Days screen

8 Click Save to close the Employee Record

SSP 8 Weeks Gross Pay

To be eligible for SSP, an employee's average weekly earnings must be above the lower earnings limit for National Insurance Contributions. Average weekly earnings are calculated by Sage Payroll from the previous eight weeks' pay. To view and check an employee's SSP 8 weeks' gross pay, do the following:

 Select your employee, and from their Employee Record click the Absence tab

 Click the S.S.P. button

3 Details of Tax Week, Tax Month, Gross Pay and date when updated are displayed

When recording previous sickness you must:

1 – enter gross pay received prior to the previous sickness,

2 – enter PIW date, and

3 – record payments made to the employee in the eight weeks prior to that date.

SSP can then be calculated if qualifying conditions are met.

Statutory Sick Pay ✕

8 Weeks Gross	Qualifying Days	Previous PIW

Payment History

Start of P.I.W. 04/12/2016

TW	TM	Gross Pay	Updated
26	6	338.00	03/10/2016
27	7	338.00	10/10/2016
28	7	338.00	17/10/2016
29	7	338.00	24/10/2016
30	7	338.00	31/10/2016
31	8	338.00	07/11/2016
32	8	338.00	14/11/2016
33	8	338.00	21/11/2016
34	8	338.00	28/11/2016

Manual entries in the table count as one week's pay.

Note: Greyed out rows either correspond to actual payments, or would conflict with the next update (based on the current processing date).

8 Weeks Average Earnings

Auto Calc   338.0000

Payments used in Calculation

No. of Payments   8

Total Payments   2704.00

The last payment detected prior to the start of PIW was made on 28/11/2016

OK   Close   Help

 Note that your employee's 8 Weeks Average Gross Pay is automatically calculated, as is the total value for payments made within the eight weeks

5 The number of payments up to the PIW is listed for you

6 After checking the figures to ensure that no processing error has been made in the payments shown, click OK to return to the Absence tab

The Start of P.I.W field is the first date of an unlinked PIW. It must be a minimum of four consecutive days' illness and not linked to an earlier period of sickness.

Recording Current Sickness

Absence through sickness for an employee is recorded using the Diary Entry button on the Absence tab of their Employee Record. Note that the AM/PM option is available purely for recording purposes, because half days do not count for SSP. To enter your employee's sickness details, follow the steps below:

Beware

Half days are not applicable to SSP.

1 From the Employee Record, click the Absence tab

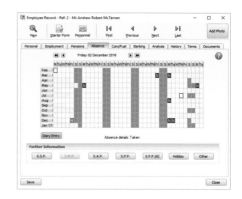

2 Click Diary Entry to record sickness

3 In Absence Type, select SSP

4 Further details can be selected to quantify the absence type

Hot tip

To produce a detailed report about SSP absences, click Reports from the Payroll toolbar and select Absence, Detailed SSP Analysis.

5 Enter inclusive dates for your employee's absence

6 Add any additional information in the Comment field

7 Click OK to save changes or Cancel to abandon

Don't forget

Absences can also be recorded by highlighting dates, clicking the right mouse button and selecting details from the pop-up options.

8 Alternative method – use the Absence tab to record all types of absence directly into the Diary. See the Hot Tip opposite

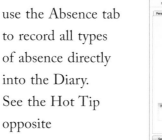

118

Entering SSP Manually

For occasions where you need to enter an employee's SSP manually, do the following:

 First, select your employee, and from their Employee Record click the Absence tab

 Click the S.S.P. button and select Qualifying Days

 Click here to enter SSP details manually

 Click OK to save and return to the Absence tab

5 Click Save and Yes to return to the Desktop

6 Next, to enter your employee's sick pay manually, click Enter Payments... from the Payroll Tasks list

7 Select the SSP/Parental Leave tab

8 Click the Recording SSP button

9 Enter your employee's SSP figure here

10 Click OK to save changes and return to the SSP window, then click Save/Next

BEFORE you can enter your employee's SSP manually you must select the Manual Statutory Sick Pay Calculations tick box on the Qualifying Days tab.

If an employee has just started work with you, the previous eight weeks' pay must be entered manually into the Gross Pay field before Sage Payroll can automatically calculate SSP.

The SSP Diary Report is useful for viewing absence details in table form and provides the employee's Qualifying Day Pattern and PIW Linkage Records.

SSP Calculation

As Government legislation often changes, it is important that you ensure all your manual and computerised information is accurate and up-to-date in order to produce the correct figures when processing your payroll.

If an employee is off sick for fewer than seven days, you can accept self-certification from them. This can be by letter, verbal or using HMRC form SC2. It should be made clear in your company policy how an employee must inform you of sickness. Note that you can only ask for a Statement of Fitness for Work, or fit note, if the employee is off sick for more than seven days.

It is important to understand how certain information is calculated if mistakes are to be avoided. Below is an example which shows you how to manually calculate SSP.

To manually calculate the amount of SSP due

The daily rate of SSP will depend upon the number of days in the week an employee is contracted to work. For example, an employee is contracted to work five days a week, i.e. Monday to Friday, and has a PIW of seven QDs and is due SSP at the standard rate of £88.45.

The SSP payable is calculated as follows:

 1 7 QDs less 3 WDs = 4 QDs for which SSP is payable

2 Daily rate of SSP is calculated as £88.45 ÷ 5 = £17.69

 3 SSP payable is £17.69 × 4 (for the 4 QDs after the 3 WDs)

4 SSP payable = £70.76

Recovering SSP

The Percentage Threshold Scheme (PTS), which allowed smaller employers to claim Statutory Sick Pay (SSP), was abolished from 6th April 2014. Under the PTS, employers were able to claim SSP where the SSP paid was more than 13% of the Class 1 NIC due for the month.

To date, therefore, it is no longer possible to recover SSP.

Regularly consult the HMRC website www.hmrc.gov.uk for up-to-date information relating to payroll legislation.

The SSP weekly rate for the payroll year 06 April 2016 to 05 April 2017 was set by Government legislation at £88.45.

Both the HMRC website and Sage Help contain examples of how to manually calculate SSP.

SSP Handy Tips

There may be times when your SSP is not calculating properly; for example, when an employee has the incorrect qualifying pattern set up. Other reasons include: the length of absence may be insufficient for the second PIW; sickness may not have been entered, where appropriate, on non-qualifying days, e.g. weekends; an employee's earnings may be below the lower earnings limit for National Insurance; the employee's 8 weeks' gross pay has not been entered; the wrong sickness date was entered accidentally, etc.

The following information shows you how to quickly check and resolve any SSP problems.

To check the employee has the correct qualifying pattern

1 From the employee's Absence tab, click the S.S.P. button

2 From the Qualifying Days tab check your employee's qualifying pattern is set correctly

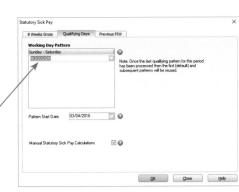

To check linked Periods of Incapacity for Work

1 From the Absence Diary check that your employee's second PIW's absence length is four or more consecutive days

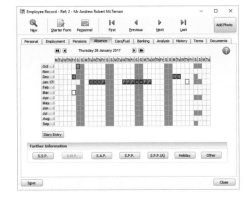

For an employee who works Monday to Friday, the Qualifying Pattern should read NQQQQQN. N is a non-qualifying day and Q is a day the employee works.

Check that the Pattern Start Date is at least the Sunday prior to the first day of sickness.

To view an employee's previous PIW, simply select their Employee Record, Absence tab, S.S.P. button and click Previous PIW.

Hot tip

Entering sickness on non-qualifying dates where appropriate ensures that ongoing periods of SSP entitlement link correctly.

Don't forget

The warning message 'Average Earnings Too Low' appears after entering SSP dates in the Absence Diary because either the employee earns below the lower earnings limit for NI or the 8 weeks' gross pay for this employee has not been entered.

...cont'd

To check and enter average earnings

1 Using the 8 Weeks Gross window from your employee's record, enter sickness start date

2 Press Tab and enter previous 8 weeks' gross pay here

3 Ensure that this figure is greater than the lower earnings limit

4 Click OK to close

To delete the wrong sickness dates before update

1 Select the incorrectly entered dates from your employee's Absence Diary

2 Click the right mouse button and select None from the drop-down list (Note the entry is now cleared.)

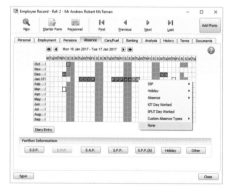

3 Click Save

10 Statutory Maternity Pay

Learn how to enter Statutory Maternity Payments, view any SMP entitlement, check employee's SMP 8 weeks' gross pay and entering SMP manually.

Introduction to SMP

Refer to Sage Payroll Help for additional information about SMP.

As long ago as 1987, a Statutory Maternity Pay scheme was introduced to provide expectant mothers with maternity pay for a maximum of 26 weeks. Payment is based upon the employee's average earnings calculated from the eight weeks' pay immediately before the Qualifying Week, and is automatically calculated for you by Sage Payroll.

Familiarise yourself with the following five SMP terms:

AWE = Average Weekly Earnings.

EWC = Expected Week of Confinement. This week starts on a Sunday.

QW = Qualifying Week. This is 15 weeks before the week the baby is due. A woman has to have been employed for 26 weeks before the QW to be eligible for SMP.

To view SMP Legislation Settings, select the Legislation option from Company toolbar, then SMP/SAP/SPP/ShPP Rates.

MPP = Maternity Pay Period (max. of 26 weeks).

MLP = Maternity Leave Period (max. of 14 weeks).

EML = Extended Maternity Leave. This can be up to 29 weeks after the birth.

To help you determine whether an employee is entitled to SMP, you should become familiar with the following:

SMP Qualifying Conditions

- Average earnings must at least equal or be above the lower earnings limit for National Insurance.
- Employee must have been continuously employed for at least 26 weeks immediately before the QW.
- Notice must be given of the date when the MPP is due to start at least 28 days beforehand.
- Has medical evidence been given of the date the baby is due within three weeks of the start of her MPP?
- Employee must still be pregnant at the 11th week before the baby is due, or have had her baby by then.
- Employee must have stopped working for you.

The employee must satisfy all six conditions to qualify for SMP, whether or not she wishes to return to work after the baby's birth.

SMP Processing Checklist

When getting ready to process any SMP payments, use the checklist below to help you:

- Does your employee meet all the qualifying conditions?
- Have you received medical evidence from your employee, including the date the baby is due?
- Your employee needs to give notice of the date her MPP is due to start at least 28 days beforehand.
- Has your employee been continuously employed by you for 26 weeks before the qualifying weeks?
- Check that your employee's last eight weeks' average earnings are not less than the lower earnings limit for National Insurance.
- Calculate your employee's qualifying week and enter it onto the system using the SMP tab.
- Has the employee now stopped working for you?

As an example, to manually calculate the amount of SMP due to an employee you would proceed as in the example below:

An employee's Average Weekly Earnings in the Qualifying Week are £400. A higher rate of SMP is calculated as 90% of average weekly earnings:

i.e. 90% x £400.00 = £360.00

This higher rate of SMP is payable for six weeks:

i.e. 6 x £360.00 = £2,160.00

The lower rate of SMP is then payable for remaining 20 weeks:

i.e. 20 x £139.58 = £2,791.60

Note: SMP payable is £139.58 from 5 April 2016 or 90% of the employee's AWE (whichever is lower) for the remaining weeks.

Therefore, the total SMP payable is:

£2,160.00 + £2,791.60 = £4,951.60

Your Sage program will tell you if your employee's average earnings are too low to claim SMP.

The Qualifying Week is the week commencing the Sunday prior to the 15 weeks before the baby is due (Expected Week of Confinement). Sage Payroll automatically records this date from the EWC date you enter in the SMP dates tab.

The higher rate of SMP is payable for 6 weeks and the lower rate of SMP is then payable for the remaining 20 weeks.

Entering Maternity Pay Details

Refer to Chapter 7 for information on processing SMP.

To ensure your employee receives the correct amount of Statutory Maternity Pay, it is important that the correct dates are recorded. To enter your employee's details once all the information is available, follow the steps below:

1 Select your employee, and from their Employment Record click Absence, then the S.M.P. button

2 From the Statutory Maternity Pay window, click the Dates tab and enter date baby is due (Expected)

3 When known, enter baby's actual date of birth

4 Enter the date employee will leave to take MPP

5 Enter this date once employee has returned to work

6 If employee has worked during the MPP, enter the number of full or part weeks in the appropriate field

7 Auto Calc will generate Average Weekly Earnings

8 Click the tick box only if you need to enter employee payments manually

9 Click OK to save

The baby's arrival date needed for the Expected On (EWC) field is normally found on the Mat B1 maternity certificate given to your employee by the midwife.

Note: If the employee's baby is born before the Expected On (EWC) date, ensure that the 'MPP started by early birth' box is checked so that employee receives correct SMP entitlement.

Viewing SMP Entitlement

The Entitlement tab displays information about an employee's Statutory Maternity Pay. It details the start of the employee's Maternity Pay Period, the total SMP entitlement and the sum amount currently due. To view SMP entitlement, do as follows:

1 From your selected Employee Record, select the Absence tab and then click the S.M.P. button

2 Select the Entitlement tab in the Statutory Maternity Pay window

3 Note the first Sunday of the Qualifying Week here

4 The start date of Maternity Pay Period is displayed for you

5 Any Previously Paid or Currently Due SMP payment details are also listed, if applicable

6 Note the Entitlement, i.e. number of Weeks, Rate and Amount, is calculated for you by Sage Payroll

7 To ensure that no data entry error has been made, it is advisable to manually calculate entitlement and check your answer agrees with the value shown as the total amount of SMP the employee is entitled to

8 Click OK to return to the Employee Record

Once an employee has received the full SMP entitlement, the program will stop calculating any further SMP.

An employee's cumulative values for SMP are stored with the Employee Record, YTD Values and are updated during payroll processing.

If you are processing an employee's payment, you can quickly view their SMP entitlement by clicking the S.M.P. button from the Absence tab on the Employee Record and selecting Entitlement.

127

SMP 8 Weeks Gross Pay

Once the employee's SMP dates have been entered, Sage Payroll uses these dates to automatically calculate the Statutory Maternity Pay entitlement. The program also establishes the employee's entitlement by checking and using the employee's 8 weeks' gross pay figures. To check an employee's SMP 8 weeks' gross pay, do the following:

Don't forget

Qualifying Week is 15 weeks before the week the baby is due. A woman has to have been employed for 26 weeks before the QW to be eligible for SMP.

1 Open the Employee's Record

2 Click on the Absence tab

3 Click the S.M.P. button to bring up the Statutory Maternity Pay window and select the 8 Weeks Gross tab

4 The date of the first Sunday in the Qualifying week appears here

Don't forget

Sage Payroll automatically enters gross earnings for you from previously processed payrolls.

128

5 The Gross average weekly payment is shown in the Gross Pay field

6 The Payment History displays the total gross pay for this employee for each tax week/month for the eight tax weeks up to and inclusive of the Qualifying Date

Hot tip

The field TW (tax week) is displayed in ascending order and includes eight tax weeks up to and including the actual Qualifying Week.

7 Note the date of the last payroll update is shown in case there has been an error and you need to perform a Rollback

8 When finished, click OK to return to the Absence window

Entering Maternity Pay Manually

When you need to enter your employee's maternity pay manually, follow the steps below:

1 Select your employee, and from their Employee Record, click the Absence tab

2 Click the S.M.P. button to bring up the Statutory Maternity Pay window

3 Select the Dates tab

4 Check that all the relevant fields are completed and tick boxes are set correctly

5 Auto Calc will generate calculated average earnings for you when appropriate

6 Click in the Manual Statutory Maternity Pay Calculations box to manually enter your SMP. Note that the Shared Parental Pay section now appears

7 After checking all the entries carefully, click OK to save any changes and return to the Absence tab

8 Click Save on the Employee Record and Close to return to the Payroll Desktop

9 Next, to manually enter the Maternity Pay, select the employee, and from the Payroll Tasks list, click on Enter Payments...

When entering maternity pay manually, you must always tick the Manual Statutory Maternity Pay Calculations box on their Employee Record BEFORE you can start processing any payments.

If the Payroll program is being used for the first time, you can manually enter the 8 weeks' gross pay prior to the Qualifying Week to satisfy the employee's entitlement to SMP.

The Payments tab on the Enter Payments window retains payment information from the previous pay period, so you could easily make a mistake if you do not check the figures.

...cont'd

If, after setting up your Employee Record to accept manual SSP payments (page 129) you then wish to process this payment, you must still follow the normal processing procedures, i.e. change Process Date to correct date, and ensure you have selected your employee BEFORE clicking Enter Payments... on the Payroll Tasks list.

Hot tip

Use the Information tab to view all payment details for an employee, i.e. Income Tax, National Insurance, Statutory Payments and Pension.

 10 Click on the Summary tab

 11 Click on the Statutory Maternity Pay finder button

12 Enter your employee's SMP figure in the next window, e.g. £180.00 for this weekly paid employee

13 Click OK to save changes and return to the Summary tab

14 Review the SMP details and pay changes. The SMP figure you entered is now displayed in the Summary

15 Click Save/Next to record your entry

This SMP is now stored with the employee's pay record.

SMP Recovery and SMP Messages

SMP Recovery

It is usually possible for most employers to reclaim 92% of the SMP, Paternity, Adoption and Shared Parental Pay they have paid out to their employees, or even 103% if your business qualifies for Small Employers' Relief. Refer to the **www.gov.uk** website for details on how to recover SMP.

To view SMP Rates

 From the Company Tasks list, select Legislation...

 Click SMP/SAP/SPP/ShPP to view legislative settings

KIT stands for Keep in Touch days. Your employee is entitled to 10 "keep in touch" days during her maternity leave. This means she can work a maximum of 10 days without it affecting her SMP. Should your employee work more than 10 days, she will lose SMP entitlement for each additional week worked.

Legislation Settings - 2016/2017

| PAYE | NI Bands & Rates | SSP | SMP/SAP/SPP/ShPP | Car Details | Student | AEO Rates | Minimum Wage | Childcare | Automatic Enrolment |

SMP Rates

Higher Rate Percentage	90.00
The standard rate is the lesser of (£)	139.58
or (%)	90.00
Higher Rate Percentage	90.00
The standard rate is the lesser of (£)	139.58
or (%)	90.00

SPP/SPP(A) Rate

The rate is the lesser of (£)	139.58
or (%)	90.00

This rate applies to both Ordinary and Additional SPP.

ShPP Rate

The rate is the lesser of (£)	139.58
or (%)	90.00

Upper Limits

Weeks payable at the higher SMP Rate	6
Weeks payable at the standard SMP Rate	33
Weeks payable at the higher SAP Rate	6
Weeks payable at the standard SAP Rate	33
Weeks payable for SPP/SPP(A)	2
Weeks payable for Additional SPP/SPP(A)	19
Weeks payable for ShPP	37
KIT Days	10
SPLiT Days	20

NIC Reclaim

Employer	Percentage Reclaimable	Compensation Percentage
Standard	92.00	0.00
Small	100.00	3.00

The Legislation Settings shown are for the 2016/2017 Tax Year

[OK] [Cancel]

---

3 Always ensure you allow your Sage Payroll program to check for any legislative updates. The values shown in the above image were current at the time of writing, but may change in the future. When done, click Cancel to exit

SMP warning messages

When there is a problem calculating SMP, Sage Payroll will display a warning message. The following are typical examples:

Sage message: Employment end date missing or less than start date

You must enter the employee's last day of work in the Ended work for MPP box or ensure the date entered is after your current processing date. Check your processing date is correctly set up.

Where an employee is not eligible for SMP, you will need to complete and give them a form SMP1 to claim Maternity Allowance from the Jobs and Benefits office. This can also now be completed online.

Save time correcting your mistakes by taking regular payroll backups which can then be restored using the File, Restore option.

...cont'd

Sage message: Employee Is Still Working
SMP cannot be paid until your employee has stopped working. Check you have correctly recorded the date they left.

Sage message: Employment Less Than 26 Weeks
An employee must be employed continuously by your company for 26 weeks prior to the qualifying date to be entitled to SMP.

Sage message: Average Earnings Too Low
Your employee's pay must at least equal or be above the National Insurance lower earnings limit to qualify for SMP.

Sage message: Previously paid SMP is shown on the Entitlement tab
Where an employee has had more than one child, Sage Payroll stores previous SMP weeks paid information. These values can be removed, if necessary, as shown below:

To zero out the SMP figures

1 From your employee's Employee Record, click the Employment tab

2 Click the YTD Values button

3 Select the Statutory Payments tab

4 Clear SMP values here

5 Click OK to save and return to the Employment tab

11 Company Pension Scheme

Learn how to set up company pension scheme details and assign a pension scheme to an employee.

Company Pension Schemes

When all employed earners reach retirement age, they are entitled to receive the basic State Pension. Prior to 6 April 2016, employees who paid Class 1 NI contributions were also entitled to an additional State Pension, but this has now changed. Under the new State Pension, your employee's National Insurance record before 6 April 2016 is used to calculate their 'starting amount'.

Also, employers are now expected to offer their employees the opportunity to join a company or occupational pension scheme, (also called a Workplace Pension). These schemes provide much better benefits on retirement than the State's basic pension. You fulfil your employer obligations by operating a pension scheme that meets the conditions specified by the Pensions Regulator.

There are many different types of pension schemes available, each with specific rules on how they operate. Once set up, Sage 50 Payroll will automatically deduct pension contributions when you pay your employees. You can use the standard schemes within Payroll, or create your own, to calculate both employee and employer pension contributions. To view a summary of pension schemes already set up in your Payroll program, do the following:

 On the Company Tasks list, click Pension Schemes...

 Various Pensions appear in the Pension Schemes window

Don't forget

You must keep your employees' pension contributions up-to-date. Any changes to the scheme must be recorded, i.e. joiners and leavers, amendments to employees and employer's contributions.

134

Don't forget

For National Insurance purposes, pension contributions and AVCs (Additional Voluntary Contributions) are not deducted from gross pay prior to calculating NI contributions for the employer and employee.

3 Click Close when finished viewing

The new State Pension

Government legislation often changes but these details about the new State Pension were correct at the time of writing:

The new State Pension is a regular payment from the Government that a person is entitled to when they reach State Pension age on or after 6 April 2016. The current rate of the full new State Pension is £155.65 per week.

To qualify for the new State Pension the person must be eligible and:

- a man born on or after 6 April 1951
- a woman born on or after 6 April 1953

Anyone who reached State Pension age before 6 April 2016 will get the State Pension under the old rules instead.

A person can still get a State Pension if they also have other income, like a personal pension, a workplace pension or are working.

Their National Insurance record is used when calculating the new State Pension for a person, so it is important for you, as an employer, to ensure that your employee's payroll is (and always has been) correctly processed. The amount they will get can be higher or lower depending on their National Insurance record. It will only be higher if they have over a certain amount of Additional State Pension.

Usually, 10 qualifying years are needed for someone to get any new State Pension.

Depending upon their total annual income, a person still working for you may have to pay tax on their State Pension. However, as State Pension payments are not taxable, HMRC will do the calculations and provide you with a suitable tax code to ensure any additional tax due by that employee is collected through PAYE.

Employees making voluntary contributions (AVCs)

Where an employer provides an occupational pension scheme, rules, conditions and benefits must be clearly defined. Where an employee decides to pay AVCs into the pension scheme, these are treated the same as the pension contributions and are deducted from gross pay before tax is calculated.

State Pension legislation changed from 6 April 2016. Read the notes on this page and refer to the **www.gov.uk** website to fully familiarise yourself with the new State Pension details.

Sage Payroll allows you to have a number of different pension schemes which you can assign to your employees. These schemes can be either a fixed amount or a percentage contribution.

Pension Scheme Checklist

Before you can start setting up a pension scheme in Sage Payroll, you need to gather certain information and details to hand and also to ensure you understand fully what type of scheme it is and how it operates.

As there are many qualifying types of pension schemes, use the following checklist to determine what type of pension scheme your company has or what schemes your employees may be already paying into.

Getting started pension checklist

- What is the scheme contribution type – a percentage or a fixed amount?
- If the pension contributions are percentage contributions, are they calculated on all elements of gross pay or just certain payments?
- If the pension contributions are of a fixed amount, are SSP and SMP payments to also be included in the pension calculation?
- If the pension contributions are a percentage, are they to be restricted by the National Insurance limits?
- Check if the pension contributions are subject to the Contracted Out Money Purchase Scheme (COMPS) or any other similar scheme?
- Has an employee reached State Pension age – they don't have to stop working but they will no longer have to pay National Insurance. Have they provided you with a Certificate of Age Exception from HMRC?
- Is your pension amount subject to tax relief?

Your company pensions advisor will be able to answer any questions you may have, if you are still unclear as to the exact details of any pension scheme or schemes your company may offer. For more information, you can also contact a pensions advisor or visit The Pensions Advisory Service website (**www.pensionsadversoryservice.org.uk**).

With Sage 50 Payroll, you can subscribe to the Pensions Module. This gives you a number of additional options, making processing automatic enrolment even easier, but there is a fee for this module.

Pensions can be a complicated payroll issue, so make sure you have all the information available and understand pensions fully before setting up your pensions information, as correcting mistakes may prove difficult.

136

If you have queries regarding pension contributions, check with your pension adviser BEFORE setting up your company pension details.

Refer to page 95 for details of how to manually enter your employees' pension payments.

Setting up Pension Schemes

Once you have all the relevant information to hand, you are ready to set up or edit your company pension schemes. For example, to edit a template to set up a Stakeholder pension for an employee already paying into one before the changes, do the following:

1 On the Company Tasks list, click Pension Schemes... to bring up the templates provided by Sage

2 Select the existing scheme you wish to change and click Edit

3 Enter a Description and select Type

Pension Schemes

Ref	Description	Type	SCON	Provider
1	Pension Scheme (1)	Other		
2	PPP Pension Scheme (2)	PPP		Prudent...
3	COMP Pension Scheme (3)	COMP	2342344C	
4	COSR Pension Scheme (4)	COSR	2343212L	
5	Pension Scheme (5)	Other		
6	Pension Scheme (6)	Other		
7	Pension Scheme (7)	Other		
8	Pension Scheme (8)	Other		

New   Edit   Delete

Enrolment Review Date / /
Payroll Id

Close

Pension

Details | Employee | Employer | Provider

Scheme Details

Reference 5
Description Stakeholder Pension Scheme
Type Other
- Other
- COMP
- COSR
- CISR
- COMB
- GPP
- PPP
- Stakeholder
- Master Trust

SCON
Qualifying Sche
Use Qualifying
pensionable pa
Scheme minimu
(Total of Ee an
Minimum Employment Period 0
(Months)
Salary Sacrifice Scheme ☐ ❓

OK   Cancel   Help

4 Click the Provider tab

5 Enter Pension Provider details in this window

Pension

Details | Employee | Employer | Provider

Provider Details

Provider
Name
Address

Post Code
Telephone
Facsimile
E-Mail
Contact
Providers Ref.
Scheme Ref.

Provider Payment Details

Sort Code 00-00-00 A/C No
Bank A/C Type Bank Account
B/Soc Roll No.
Payment Method Cheque

Administrator Details

Name
E-Mail
Telephone

OK   Cancel   Help

...cont'd

6 Click the Employee tab

7 Select Fixed Amount or Percentage from drop-down list

8 Enter the contribution value here

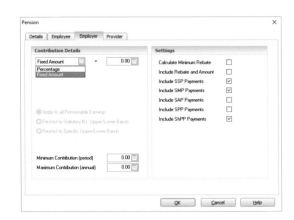

9 Complete the remaining Details and Settings relevant to the type of scheme you have selected

10 Click the Employer tab

Don't forget

The Restrict to Specific Upper/Lower Bands option allows you to set your own defined earnings limit. Once selected, you can enter your own earning limits into the Lower and Upper limits boxes which appear automatically.

11 Enter the Employer Contribution Details as you did for the employee, then click OK to save

Assigning Pension Schemes

Once the pension schemes have been set up, you can now assign the appropriate scheme to your employees, either individually or as a group, as follows:

To assign a pension scheme to an individual employee

 1 Select and open your employee's record by double-clicking on the employee with the left mouse button

2 Select the Pensions tab and click the Manage Schemes button

3 Click the Add button

4 Use the Finder button and select the relevant pension scheme

5 Click OK

6 Click OK to save details

To quickly create a new pension scheme you can simply select and edit one of the existing templates provided.

139

To assign a pension scheme to a group of employees

1 Select relevant employees from the Employee List, then from the Tasks menu, choose Global Changes, Pensions and Add Pension

2 Select the pension scheme from the drop-down list, then click OK and Yes to continue

You cannot delete a pension scheme that is currently still assigned to an employee.

Additional Voluntary Contributions

The amount of AVC contributions you can make each year is limited. Refer enquiries to your pension adviser or the **www.gov.uk** website pages.

Where an employee is a member of a company pension scheme they can choose to make additional contributions. For example, they may want to pay an additional £50 a month into their pension. Sage Payroll allows you to process any Additional Voluntary Contributions (AVCs) your employees choose to make to their company scheme.

To process AVCs, do the following:

1 Select and open your employee's record by double-clicking on the employee with the left hand mouse button

2 Select Pensions tab and click the Manage Schemes button

3 Select the Pension Scheme and click Edit

Pension	✕

Pension Details / Pension Information

Scheme Reference	4	Description	COSR Pension Scheme (4)
Employee Pension Reference		Type	COSR
Qualifying Scheme	☐ ❓	SCON	2343212L

Joined Scheme ❓	02/12/2016	Provider Notified ☐	Contractual ☐ ❓
Active Membership Achieved	02/12/2016		
Left Scheme ❓	/ /	Provider Notified ☐	

Employee Contributions	Fixed Amount = 20.00
Additional Voluntary Contributions	Fixed Amount = 0.00
	Percentage
Employer Contributions	Fixed Amount =

Calculator: `< C Ce /` `7 8 9 *` `4 5 6 -` `1 2 3 +` `0 . =`

Primary Scheme ☑   OK   Cancel   Help

The AVC is currently subject to tax relief.

4 Select the type of AVC, Fixed Amount or Percentage

5 Enter the Amount of contribution, using the calculator if necessary

6 Click OK to save the AVC details

7 Close any remaining windows

12 Deductions, Loans and Attachments

This chapter shows you how to set up different types of deductions, loans and attachments of earnings. Once set up, you will learn how to allocate these against your employees, and the processing of deductions during the payroll run.

Setting up Deductions

Within Sage Payroll you are allowed to set up as many deduction types as you require. Once your deductions have been set up, they can be assigned to your employees and automatically deducted from your employees' pay as part of normal payroll processing. To set up your deduction types, do as follows:

Don't forget

Status can be set to Variable (no restrictions for when rates/hours need changing), Fixed (rate/amounts are fixed by value entered in each Employee Record), or Global (any changes made to payments will directly affect all employees who have been assigned to it). To change it, use the Pay Elements Settings.

142

1 From the Company Tasks list, click Pay Elements...

2 Click the Deductions tab

3 Click the New button to create a new deduction type

4 Select Status from the drop-down list

5 Enter a description

6 Enter the default number of hours

7 Enter the default rate

8 Click any appropriate deductions

9 Click OK to save changes or Close to abandon

Don't forget

It is usually advisable to leave the Default Hours/No and Rate at zero unless all your employees work the same hours.

Allocating Deduction Types

Once deduction types have been set up, you can assign them to your employees following the steps below:

 1 Select your employee, and from their Employee Record select the Employment tab

Press Function key F1 for further information on the relevant screens.

2 Click the Pay Elements button

3 From the Pay Elements window, click the Deductions tab

4 Click here for a deduction list

5 Select the desired deduction

6 Click OK to accept

7 Enter figures as required in the next window

Press the Tab key to move right across columns and Shift + Tab to move left.

8 Repeat Steps 3-7 to add another deduction type if necessary

9 Click Save to close or Cancel to abandon

The Tax field displays Pre or Post to indicate whether the deduction is to be made before or after tax is calculated.

Processing Deductions

Before processing deductions for your employees, values may need assigning for specific variable deductions using the Deductions tab from the Enter Payments window. Popular deduction types include payments for union fees, recreation activities etc. To enter values and process your deductions, do as follows:

Hot tip

If a default number has already been set up for the deduction type in the Hours/No field, it appears automatically. Likewise for the Rate and Amount field values.

 Select your employee from the Employee List and click on the Enter Payments... option on the Payroll Tasks list

2 From the Enter Payments window, click Deductions

3 Deduction types previously assigned to the employee are displayed

 Enter number of hours or the number of deduction payments here

Enter Payments - Ref: 2 - Mr Andrew Robert McTernan								— □ ×

Employee | First | Previous | Find | Select | Next | Last

Payments | **Deductions** | Attachments | Loans | SSP/Parental Leave | Summary | Information | Notes

Deduction Name	Tax	NI	Hours/No	Rate	Amount
Professional Subscription	Pre	Post	1.0000	50.0000	50.00
Union	Post	Post	1.0000	14.7800	14.78
Christmas Fund	Post	Post	1.0000	5.0000	5.00

Add Deduction

Tax Code		Gross Pay	No of Adv. Periods	Advanced Pay	PAYE	NIC	Net Pay
749L		338.00	0	0.00	0.00	22.02	246.20

Advance Pay | Holiday Fund | Employer's | Foreign Tax

Select this check box if your employee is leaving and this is their final payment ☐

Save / Next | Close

09/03/2017 Week 49 | 2016/2017

5 Enter the deduction rate for the deduction type

6 To add new deductions, return to the Employee Record and do Steps 2-9 on page 143

7 Check that all deductions have been recorded accurately then click Save/Next to move to the next record

Don't forget

You can view total value of deductions paid per employee using the Payments and Deductions tab from the YTD Values window.

Advancing Deductions

For occasions where you may need to process an employee's deductions in advance, for example, their holiday period, you can do this following the steps below:

1 Select your employee and click Enter Payments... from the Payroll Tasks list

2 Click on the Advance Pay button

Hot tip

Use the Summary tab to view Pre-tax and Post-tax Deductions for both Current and Advanced pay periods.

3 Enter the number of payments that you are advancing, i.e. number of weeks or number of months

4 Complete the Payment details

5 Click OK

6 Click the Deductions tab

Hot tip

To print out deduction information, use the Reports option, Employee folder, Employee Details – Deductions report.

7 Enter the employee's deductions details and click Save

Beware

For employees who owe different loan amounts or the repayment deductions vary, amend their individual Employee Record when assigning the loan.

Beware

What facilities are available in your Payroll program depends on which version of Sage Payroll you are using.

Setting up Loans

Where a company provides loans for their employees, these can be set up and assigned to the employee's record card. The loan repayments will then be automatically deducted from the employee's pay. To set up your loan types, do as follows:

1 From the Company Tasks list, click Pay Elements...

2 Click the Loans tab

3 Click New to create a new loan type

4 Enter a suitable loan Description

5 Enter the default loan amount

6 Enter the amount to be deducted from pay to repay the loan

7 Click in the Transfer to Sage P11D box if applicable

8 Click OK to save changes or Close to abandon

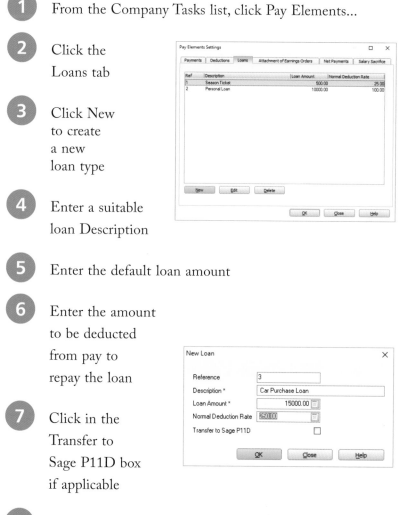

Note: The Loans facility may not available to users of some versions of Sage Payroll software.

Allocating Loans

Once loan types have been set up, you can assign them to your employees following the steps below:

 1 Select your employee, and from their Employee Record select the Employment tab

2 Click the Pay Elements button

3 From the Pay Elements window, click the Loans tab

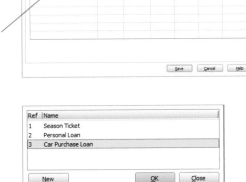

4 Click here for a loans list

5 Select the required loan

6 Click OK to accept

7 You can amend the Normal Deduction Rate if required

8 Repeat Steps 3-7 to add another deduction as required

9 Click Save to close or Cancel to abandon

Beware

If the normal Deduction Rate field is blank, you must enter the values manually every time you process the payroll.

Don't forget

Where an employee makes an additional loan repayment which is not part of the payroll routine, the Amount Paid To Date field needs amending to record this.

Hot tip

The Status field displays "Active" until the Balance Outstanding is zero, when Status displays "Paid". However, the loan Status may also be changed to "Written Off".

Processing Loans

Loan repayment details are normally set up on your employee's individual record card. However, certain values may be entered or amended using the Enter Payments window. To enter values and process your loan repayments, do as follows:

 Select your employee from the Employee list and click Enter Payments... from the Payroll Tasks list

 From the Enter Payments window, click Loans

 Any loans assigned to that employee are listed

 The Repayment Made and Balance Carried Forward values will be calculated automatically

Enter Payments - Ref: 2 - Mr Andrew Robert McTernan						
Employee	First	Previous	Find	Select	Next	Last

Payments | Deductions | Attachments | Loans | SSP/Parental Leave | Summary | Information | Notes

Description	Balance Brought Forward	Repayment Due	Repayment Made	Balance Carried Forward
Car Purchase Loan	15000.00	250.00	0.00	15000.00

Add Loan

Tax Code	Gross Pay	No of Adv. Periods	Advanced Pay	PAYE	NIC	Net Pay
749L	75.00	1	450.00	12.50	35.46	-57.74

Advance Pay | Holiday Fund | Employer's | Foreign Tax

Select this check box if your employee is leaving and this is their final payment ☐

Save / Next | Close

06/01/2017 | Week 40 | 2016/2017

 If required, enter a new value in the Repayment Due field

 To add new loans, click the Employee button to return to the Employee Record, then follow Steps 2-8 on page 147

7 Check that all loans have been recorded accurately then click Save/Next to close, or move to next record

Attachment of Earnings

An Attachment of Earnings Order is an official form issued by a court and is legally binding to an employer instructing them to deduct an outstanding debt from an employee's wages. These Attachments are always taken from the employees' net pay, referred to as Attachable Earnings.

The court sets a Protected Earnings Amount to ensure that the employee has sufficient income after deductions have been made. The difference between the protected and attachable earnings is the sum from which the deduction is actually made.

These payments are usually on a weekly or monthly basis. Examples of these orders include the non payment of council tax, fines and child support payments, etc.

Sage automatically provides you with a list of Attachments. A user can add or edit these descriptions where appropriate and later assign them to an employee's details. To view these Attachments, do the following:

Employers are allowed to deduct an admin fee from their employees for administering any Attachment of Earnings. If an Attachment is subject to an administration fee, the amount deducted appears. The administration fee is only deducted once for each Attachment type.

1 From the Company Tasks list, click Pay Elements...

2 Click the Attachments of Earnings Orders tab

3 A list of standard Attachment types appears

4 You can type in your own Replacement Description. This will appear on reports and payslips

5 Click OK to save or Close to abandon any changes you made

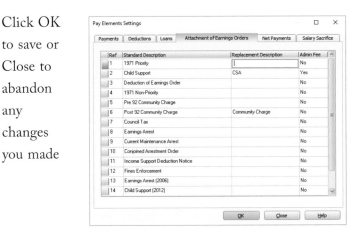

Pay Elements Settings

Payments | Deductions | Loans | **Attachment of Earnings Orders** | Net Payments | Salary Sacrifice

Ref	Standard Description	Replacement Description	Admin Fee
1	1971 Priority		No
2	Child Support	CSA	Yes
3	Deduction of Earnings Order		No
4	1971 Non-Priority		No
5	Pre 92 Community Charge		No
6	Post 92 Community Charge	Community Charge	No
7	Council Tax		No
8	Earnings Arrest		No
9	Current Maintenance Arrest		No
10	Conjoined Arrestment Order		No
11	Income Support Deduction Notice		No
12	Fines Enforcement		No
13	Earnings Arrest (2006)		No
14	Child Support (2012)		No

OK | Close | Help

Within Sage Payroll you can determine which attachment is to be deducted first, for example, Maintenance Orders and Community Charge Orders have a higher priority than civil debt deductions.

150

Don't forget

An employee is allocated a Protected Earnings figure, i.e. a minimum net pay. The Attachment cannot deduct all their earnings. If earnings are below the protected level the deduction will not be made. If the order is a protected order, any arrears will be carried forward to the next period. Non-protected orders do not carry forward arrears.

...cont'd

Descriptions for the most commonly used attachments

To help you, here is a list of the more common attachments you are likely to come across whilst processing payroll. Their templates are already pre-defined in Sage Payroll:

1971 Priority:	This refers to a priority court order, e.g. road traffic fine or non payment of television licence.
Child Support:	Deduction to cover child maintenance payments.
DEO:	Deduction of Earnings Order. A Scottish child support order.
1971 Non-Priority:	This is a non-priority order, e.g. money owing on an unpaid credit card or for work done.
Pre 92 CCAEO:	A deduction to recover missing community charge payments from before April 1992 (poll tax).
Post 92 CCAEO:	This deduction is to recover missing community charge payments after April 1992 (now council tax).
Council Tax:	This is a current council tax order.
Earnings Arrest:	This is a Scottish order, an earnings arrestment order, e.g. a fine or civil debt.
CMA:	This is a current maintenance arrestment to cover maintenance after a marriage separation/divorce.
CAO:	A combined arrestment order, e.g. maintenance, and earnings arrest.
ISDN:	This refers to Student Loans and Income Support Deduction notices.
Fines Enforcement:	Issued to ensure court fines are paid.
Earnings Arrest (2006):	A Scottish order, bankruptcy and diligence.
Child Support 2012:	From April 2012, issued by the (CSA) for child maintenance payments.

Allocating Attachments

For employees who are required to pay an Attachment of
Earnings Order, follow the steps below:

1 Select your employee and from their Employment Record,
click on the Employment tab

2 Click the Pay Elements button

3 Click the Attachments tab

4 Click here
and select the
attachment
required from
the drop-
down list

In the Priority Order
field, where more than
one attachment needs
deducting enter 1 for the
highest priority, then 2
as next priority, etc.

Where only one
attachment is entered
you must enter 1 into
the Priority Order field.
Field entry is mandatory.

5 Enter Priority
Order number

6 Enter Normal
Deduction Rate

7 Enter Protected Earnings amount

8 Enter Total Attachment amount

9 Enter the date the court order was issued

10 Enter a court reference number in the
Order Reference field

11 Tick to use pre-defined tables, if appropriate to this
Attachment of Earnings Order, then click Save

Don't forget

The Amount/Percent field shows if the attachment is to be calculated as a percentage of the employee's wages or as a fixed amount.

Hot tip

Use the Advance Pay button to process an employee's attachments in advance.

Processing Attachments

Sage Payroll will process these Attachments of Earnings automatically for those employees liable for these deductions. To process these attachments, follow the steps below:

 Select the employee and click Enter Payments... from the Payroll Tasks list

 Select the Attachments tab. This shows any attachments that have been set up for this employee

 To add a new attachment you need to click the Employee button and then follow Steps 1-12 on page 151

4 The Attach Value shows the amount being deducted

5 The Attach Earnings field shows the earnings from which the attachment is deducted

 Note the actual Amount Deducted, which takes into account any protected earnings

 Click Save/Next to save and move to next record or Close to return to the Payroll Desktop

Note: If the whole amount is unable to be processed for this period, the Amount CF field shows the value carried forward to the next period. The Protd CF field shows any protected earnings which are also carried forward.

13 Working Online

You should have an active internet connection when working in Payroll.

154

Remember to regularly check if your software is up-to-date or whether updates need installing.

Hot tip

Sage will prompt you to check if your software is up-to-date when you run certain tasks.

Software Updates

A convenient feature of Sage 50 Payroll is the ability to download and install updates, thus ensuring that both your software and Government legislation remain fully up-to-date at all times.

To make use of this feature you must ensure that you have an active internet connection so that your program can connect to the Sage server. You can update manually or let Payroll ask if you wish to check for updates when performing certain tasks that rely on legislation being current.

To update manually

 On the Payroll main menu, select Help, Check For Updates

 Wait for Payroll to establish contact with Sage then follow prompts to download and install any updates

 Download and install progress is displayed. Click Close when updating is complete

 If there are no new updates and your program is already up-to-date, simply click Close

To update from prompts

For some tasks, such as Enter Payments, Payroll will prompt you to check for updates before continuing, as follows:

 An Update prompt appears

Click Yes, wait for Payroll to establish contact with Sage then follow prompts to download and install any updates

e-Submission

Sage 50 Payroll can submit information directly to HMRC via the Government Gateway. In order to do this, you need to set up your e-Submission settings.

To configure for e-Submissions

 1 On the Payroll main menu, select Tasks, e-Submissions, e-Submission Settings...

 2 Enter details in the Settings and Contact Details tabs

e-Submission Settings ✕

| Settings | Contact Details |

Company Name *   Wizard Training Limited   Tax Dist./Ref. *   155 / 4341057   ❓

User ID *   DELTATO   Password *   **********

Check for new messages when opening the IR Secure Mailbox   ☑   Clear P46 (Car) flag on submission   ☐

Show FPS checklist   ☑

Mandatory fields indicated with * must be completed within both tabs before these settings can be saved.

If the Company Name or Tax Dist/Ref is incorrect you can correct them above and the company details will be updated.

Save   Close

3 When finished, click Save to record the settings and Close

To check the e-Submission version
To ensure you have the latest e-Submission module installed, simply do the following:

1 On the Payroll Help menu, select e-Submission Version Check

2 If up-to-date then click OK to close

Sage Payroll ✕

ℹ You are using the latest available version.

OK

Hot tip

To save time, have all of the details to hand before setting up your e-Submission settings.

Beware

If you are not using the latest version of the e-Submission module you will not be able to make a submission via the Government Gateway.

Cloud Working

Introduction to Cloud Computing

Cloud computing is a relatively new technology that offers many advantages that could immediately benefit a business, especially a micro or small business, due to the lower cost compared to purchasing the software outright. It also offers 24/7 access from any location in the world that has an active internet connection.

Sage offers Cloud-based computing for both Payroll and Accounting that is accessible from a PC, Mac or mobile device.

Sage One Payroll is Cloud-based software recognised by HMRC as being compliant with the latest Payroll legislation. It makes RTI submissions directly to HMRC, and automatic updates mean you will always be up-to-date with the latest changes. Dealing with workplace pension legislation is easy using a four step preparation process, from assessing your workforce to keeping your records up-to-date.

It has the same features as Sage 50 Payroll, so you can still refer to the various chapters in this book when processing your payroll.

However, as the data is held on a Sage server, you do not have to remember to ensure your program or payroll bandwidths and rates are the latest as this is looked after by Sage. You will be up-to-date every time you log in and your data files are secure.

Your Cloud-based Payroll program also features automatic integration with Sage One Start and Sage One Accounting, if you subscribe to that software as well, meaning that payroll data is always accurately recorded in your accounts. Many small businesses will find this both useful and time saving. If you are a small or micro business you should seriously consider Cloud working as a cheaper and simpler way of integrating your accounts and payroll into an easy to manage and use package.

Sage Cloud-based payroll software is usually available via monthly subscription based on 5, 10 or 15 employees. It makes running a payroll system easier and with the online help you can quickly pay your staff without any previous payroll experience. This can be ideal for owner-managers who want to control their payroll in-house.

With the change to mandatory electronic submission of payroll data to HMRC, Cloud working simplifies many of the tasks.

Hot tip

Cloud-based working allows you to access and process your employees' payroll when away from the workplace.

Hot tip

Consider Cloud computing for your accounts and payroll systems if you are a small business with less than 15 employees.

Don't forget

Cloud-based software is often cheaper to purchase than stand-alone software, plus all updates following legislation changes are handled for you.

14 The Report Designer

Learn how to create a new custom report and modify an existing report layout.

Introducing the Report Designer

Payroll reports are grouped in the following sections: Employee, Company, Legislation, Period End, Year End, Absence, Cars & Fuel, User Defined (Local) and Report Selections.

When you first install Sage Payroll, you are automatically provided with all of the reports and stationery to suit most business needs. When printing these reports, if you are using stationery supplied by Sage, the data should fit in the pre-printed stationery layouts without adjustment.

There may be occasions, though, when you need to create a new report or modify an existing one to meet your specific needs. The Report Designer lets you do all of this so you can meet any requirements your business may have. To choose a report and get started with the Report Designer, do as follows:

 Click the Reports button from the toolbar

 Select the report section you require, e.g. Company

 Choose required report from the list view

 The Reports toolbar allows you to choose whether to create New, Edit, Delete, Print, Preview, Export, Email or send the report to Excel

If you only require pre-update reports, select the Pre-update Reports option from the Payroll toolbar.

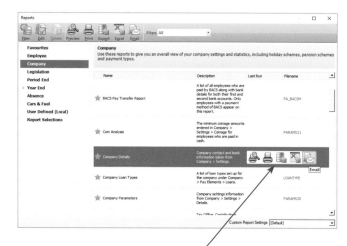

To edit an existing report, select the required layout from the Reports list view, then click the Edit option from the toolbar.

 You can also choose some of these options by pointing at the report with the mouse cursor and clicking an icon

Creating a New Report

The following example shows you how to use the Report Wizard to create an Employee report. This will display their name, date of birth, National Insurance number and address details. The report is sorted on the employee's surname and is useful for supplying details to the HMRC National Insurance Contributions and Employer Office. To create this report, follow the steps below:

Hot tip

To quickly preview a report, point to the layout you require and click the Preview button that appears.

 1 Select the Reports option from the toolbar

2 To create your Employee report, click the New button to start the Report Designer and Report Wizard

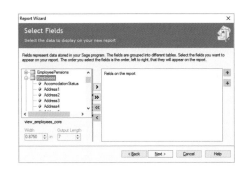

3 Select Employee in the Document Type window

4 Click Next to continue

Hot tip

You can easily send a report to someone in your Outlook contacts list by pointing to the layout you require and clicking the Email button that appears.

5 In the Select Fields window, scroll down the list of fields and double-click on Employees to bring up a further list of Employee fields

...cont'd

Hot tip

To make a selective choice of fields, hold down the Ctrl key whilst clicking on variables required. Click the Add (>) button to transfer them as a group.

Hot tip

To remove any field from the Fields on the report list, select it and use the Remove button (<). Where all variables need removing, use the Remove All button (<<).

6 Scroll down the list of employee fields and select Surname (the fields are in alphabetical order)

7 Click the Add (>) button to copy the field to the list of fields to be included on the Report

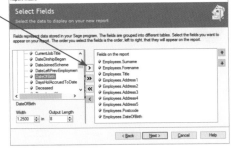

8 Repeat Step 6 and Step 7 for all the fields you require

9 When done, click Next

10 Check you have all the fields and click Next, as grouping is not required

11 Select Surname field to sort on, click the Add (>) button and choose to sort Ascending

12 Click Next twice, deselect all Criteria and click Next again

13 Give the report a name and click Finish to generate the required layout

Previewing your report

1 Click Preview to run your new report

2 To save, click File, Save As and enter file name. Note where it is saved

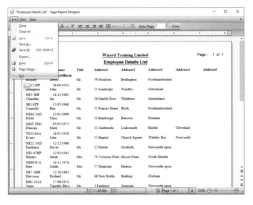

Your report will appear in the User Defined (Local) folder after you save it.

3 To Close, click on File and Exit

4 To rearrange text headings and fields, see below and page 162

Arranging your variables (fields)

The Report Wizard places all text headings and variables in the Report Designer window. These will need rearranging and positioning in the correct place using 'drag and drop'. Any unwanted headings can be removed by selecting and clicking Delete.

Fields need to be aligned to produce a neat and tidy appearance. For example, to align the Surname heading in the Page Header with the Surname field in the Details section, you need to hold down the Shift Key continuously while clicking on the two variables, drag them to the correct position and let go of the mouse button. To align multiple objects, choose Pointer (select) on the toolbar and drag a box around the objects you require. From the Format menu, select Alignment, e.g. Left, and click OK. Be careful not to move a variable from one section to another.

Use drag and drop to place fields and text headings in their correct position, i.e. click on a field or heading, hold down the left mouse button, move the mouse pointer to the required position and release the mouse button.

...cont'd

Don't forget

The Page Header normally displays the report's column headings and will print on every page of the report. The Details section contains the main body of your report information.

Don't forget

The Page Footer section prints at the bottom of every page.

Hot tip

The Report Designer helps you position fields vertically under a heading by snapping them into place for you.

1 Open the report for editing

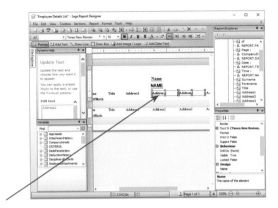

2 Remove any unnecessary text headers, i.e. Address2 to Address5 and Postcode. To do this, select the object and press Delete

3 Rearrange text headers and fields so your report layout looks like this. Use 'drag and drop'; the fields will snap in place

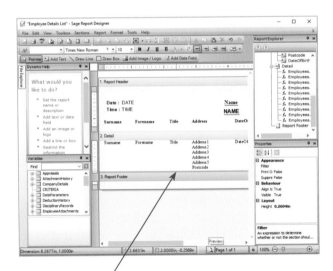

4 Click on this line and drag up or down to adjust the spacing between Employee Records

5 Click the Preview tab to check the layout

6 When satisfied with the result, move to the next section (page 163). If changes are necessary, use the Designer tab

To save and print your new report

1 From the Report Designer toolbar, select File menu

2 Click on
Save As...

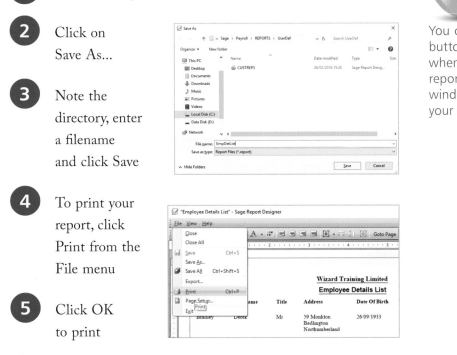

3 Note the
directory, enter
a filename
and click Save

4 To print your
report, click
Print from the
File menu

5 Click OK
to print

6 Your printed report should look similar to this:

Note: If your printed report has information missing at the top, bottom, left or right edges of the page, the report needs editing accordingly to increase the amount of space at the top, bottom and sides of your page layout.

You can use the Print button that appears when pointing to a report in the Report window to quickly print your report.

Be careful not to overwrite any existing reports. They may be useful to you later.

Modifying an Existing Report

The Report Designer lets you modify existing layout files and your program's default reports. However, with some reports you will be prompted by Sage Payroll to save them with a different filename.

To modify a laser payslip

 Select an employee and from the Payroll Tasks list click Pre-update Reports...

 Select the laser payslip report layout you want to modify from the Payslips, Laser section

 Click Edit to open the report layout

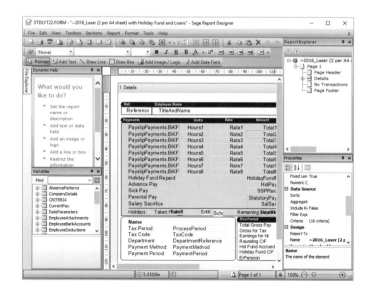

 You can make any changes you require to the report design. Use 'drag and drop', delete unwanted objects, etc.

5 For this
example, the
Salary Sacrifice
details are
going to
be removed

6 Click on fields
to be removed
and press the
Delete key

Always preview your
reports before printing.
For example, check all
headings and fields line
up correctly etc.

7 Click Preview
to check the
changes to
the layout

8 Note Salary
Sacrifice
details are
not displayed

Refer to the Sage
Payroll Report Designer,
Help Topics section for
additional information
about working with any
of your reports.

9 To save your changes, click Save As... from the File menu

10 Select the
correct directory

11 Enter a new
filename

12 Click Save

13 To print out the payslips, click Print from the
Preview window

Always remember to
save any new changes
you wish to keep.

Creating a Custom Report

Earlier you were shown how to create a new report using a single set of fields, but you can also create a report customised from different sets of fields, such as a report incorporating payments, deductions, loans and attachments. Below is an example of a report which includes employee payment history for salary, loans and deductions. To create this report, do the following:

 Select the Reports option from the toolbar

 To create your customised report, click the New button to start the Report Designer and Report Wizard

3 Select Employee and click Next

4 Scroll down to Employees and add the Surname and Initials fields to the Fields on the report list. See page 160 for adding a field

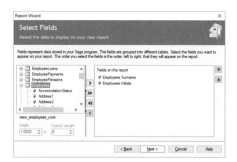

5 Now scroll down to Payment History and add the Payment Description and the Payment Amount Total to the Fields on the report list

166

...cont'd

6 Scroll down to Employee Loans and add Loan Reference and Amount Paid To Date to the Fields on the report list

7 Scroll down to Employee Deductions and add Description and Value To Date to the Fields on the report list

To copy a field across to the Field on the report list click the Add (>) button. If you wish to remove a field from the report list, use the Remove (<) button. Where all variables need removing use the Remove All (<<) button.

167

8 Click Next and Next again

9 Select the Surname field to sort on, click the Add button and choose to sort Ascending

10 Click Next

11 Remove Loan Reference from the Totals list and click Next

...cont'd

 Deselect all Criteria and click Next again

 Give the report a name and click Finish to generate the layout

 Refer to page 161 for previewing and rearranging the fields until you are happy with the layout of the report. If necessary, cancel your first attempt and try again until you get it right. This also helps you become familiar with Report Designer and working with fields, grouping, sorts, totals, criteria and report layout in general

15 Don't forget to save and print your report as shown on page 163. When saved, the report name will appear in the User Defined (Local) list in the Reports window

15 Year End Procedure

See how to run your Year End procedure using the Payroll Year End Process, learn how to finish one year and prepare for the next.

Year End Checklist

If you are unfamiliar with the process, before starting your Year End routine, work through the following list to help you become familiar with what Year End entails. This is a useful exercise if you are submitting your Year End manually.

Year End Checklist

- Run and update your final payroll period for all payment types and process any leavers without company cars.
- Process leavers with company cars.
- Remove leave dates for leavers with company cars.
- Set your process date to the Year End date, which is usually 5 April.
- Take two backups of your data and label them 'Post Update before clearing Year To Date'.
- Print P11 PAYE and P11 NIC Deductions forms.
- Check your P35 Summary against the P11 PAYE and P11 NIC.
- Print your P60s.
- Clear your employees' YTD Totals and, if required, transfer any car mileage records.
- Back up your data and label it 'After Clearing Year To Date Totals'.
- Check your Government parameters against current legislation and update them if necessary.
- Re-enter the leave dates for leavers with company cars so they are not processed again in future payroll runs.
- Enter any tax code changes for your employees.
- Remove any week 1/month 1 tax codes.

Under RTI, you no longer need to make P14 and P35 submissions at the end of the tax year. However, you need to answer some declaration questions similar to those on the P35; the Payroll Year End menu will guide you through all of the necessary steps. You must also provide your employees with their P60s by 31 May each year.

Year End Procedure

Before Government legislation made it mandatory for a business to submit payroll information online, running the Year End Procedure was quite a lengthy business. However, as reports such as pay information have to be submitted to HMRC each time you do a payroll run, Year End reporting has become simpler.

This chapter covers the production of paper reports, should you be one of the very few businesses that have qualified for exemption and do manual submissions. Whichever system you're using, first familiarise yourself with the Year End checklist on page 170, then to run your Year End procedure, follow the steps below:

Always remember to set your Process Date to the Year End date, i.e. 5 April and year.

1 From the Tasks menu select Payroll Year End

2 The program will ensure all your employees are selected, so click Yes to the prompt

3 The current Tax Year is selected for you, but you can change it here if not correct

4 If you are no longer an employer, enter date PAYE ended

Remember to distribute your P60s to your employees by 31 May.

5 Click OK to continue

6 This information message will appear if the tax year had to be changed

7 Click OK to continue to the Payroll Year End Main Menu window

...cont'd

To submit the End Of Year Declarations to HMRC

1 The Year End steps are shown. Click the Submission button to start sending your End Of Year Declarations to HMRC

2 Wait whilst contact is established with HMRC's server

3 The Employer Payment Summary Wizard opens

4 Note that once started, this process cannot be reversed. If you wish to proceed and make your submissions, click Continue, else click Close to abandon and try again later

5 Check your details are correct then click Submit to begin the submission of your data

> **Employer Payment Summary**
>
> **Check Your Details**
> The following credentials will be used by the submission process. Please ensure they are correct.
> NOTE: Any changes made will not be saved once the submission has been completed.
>
> **Gateway Registration**
> User ID   DELTATO
> Password   ***********
>
> **Company Details**
> Name   Wizard Training Limited
> Tax Office/Reference   155 / 4341057
> Accounts Office Ref.   155PB001024690512
>
> Pressing 'Submit' will begin the submission of your data.
>
> Back   Submit   Close

Don't forget

A B/F value represents cumulative figures entered manually into the Payroll system.

6 Wait for submissions to complete. If there is a problem then a warning screen appears with details. You can print this and attempt to rectify the issue. When submission is successful, a tick appears in the Main Menu window

To produce P60 Certificates

1 Click here to start producing your P60s

2 Make sure you have the correct forms for this tax year

> **Payroll Year End - 05/04/2017**   ×
>
> **Main Menu**
>
> We recommend you complete the steps in numerical order. Completed steps will be highlighted with a tick.
>
> ✔ **Step 1** Internet Submission   Use this step to submit the End of Year Declarations to HMRC electronically.
> **Step 2** Produce P60s   You must ensure you are using the correct P60 forms which show 2016/2017.
> **Step 3** Take a backup   Take at least one post year end backup of your payroll files.
> **Step 4** Complete Year End   Deletes expired historical data and cumulative values.
> **Step 5** Distribute P60s
>
> Close   Restart   Help
> Step 1 of 5   Internet Submission   05/04/2017   2016/2017

Hot tip

If you make a mistake when working through the Year End procedure, simply click Close or Restart and start again.

3 Select the type of stationery to use. It is also advisable to always do a Test Print of the P60 to ensure that the format and layout are correct before printing the actual forms to give to your employees

> **Payroll Year End - 05/04/2017**   ×
>
> **Produce P60**
>
> All employers must send their tax year end returns to HMRC electronically. Paper returns will not be accepted. Employees will require a copy of their P60.
>
> Contact Sage if you are unsure which type of stationery to use.
>
> Select the type of stationery to be used   P60 HMRC Laser
>
> Test Print   Print
>
>   Completed
> P60 HMRC Laser   Print   ☐
>
> Preview Reports before printing ☑
>
> Next Step   Close   Help
> Step 2 of 5   Produce P60s   05/04/2017   2016/2017

...cont'd

 4 When ready, click
Print here to print
the P60s

 5 Click Close
when completed

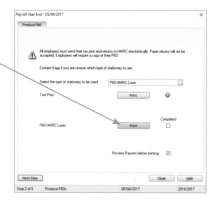

Hot tip

If an employee has a letter A displayed in the Nat Ins Category column it means they make standard contributions. A letter X is used to indicate that they are exempt, such as when they have reached retirement age and no longer have to make NI contributions.

Don't forget

Class 1A NIC due on company cars is paid one tax year in arrears. As all leavers are removed from the system during the Year End procedure, the leave date of these employees must be removed to retain the car information and then re-entered after the Year End procedure.

To take a backup

1 Click on the Step 3
backup button

2 Follow the
instructions. These
are similar to the
steps for backing
up your data files
on page 185

To complete Year End

1 Click on the Step 4
Complete Year End
icon to clear expired
historical data and
cumulative values

2 Click Yes on the
information screen
to proceed and
Complete Year End

...cont'd

Distribution of P60s

After carrying out your Year End procedure you will need to distribute the P60 certificates, by law, to each of your employees by a given date.

To remind you, the final step on the Payroll Year End Main Menu is the distribution of the P60:

Always test print a couple of P60s to check your pre-printed stationery and printer alignment is correct.

Payroll Year End - 05/04/2017 ✕

Main Menu

We recommend you complete the steps in numerical order. Completed steps will be highlighted with a tick. ✔

✔ **Step 1** Internet Submission — Use this step to submit the End of Year Declarations to HMRC electronically.

✔ **Step 2** Produce P60s — You must ensure you are using the correct P60 forms which show 2016/2017.

✔ **Step 3** Take a backup — Take at least one post year end backup of your payroll files.

✔ **Step 4** Complete Year End — Deletes expired historical data and cumulative values.

Step 5 Distribute P60s

Close Restart Help

Step 3 of 5   Take a backup   05/04/2017   2016/2017

1 Click on the Step 5 Distribute P60s button

2 Note the date you must distribute the P60s by

3 Note also the date you need to pay PAYE and NIC by for your final payroll run. The Year End is complete

Make your PAYE and NIC payments for the final payroll run to HMRC by the due date.

Payroll Year End - 05/04/2017 ✕

Distribute year end returns

You must distribute the P60s to your employees by 31 May 2017.

You must make payment of PAYE and NIC deductions for your final payroll run by 19 April 2017.

Congratulations! As long as you have completed all of the steps detailed in the Payroll Year End menu, you have successfully completed your year end. If you have not already done so you can now install your new payroll update program for the 2017/2018 tax year. Installing your new program will reset the Payroll Year End process by removing the ticks next to each completed task.

Close Restart Help

Step 5 of 5   Distribute P60s   05/04/2017   2016/2017

...cont'd

More information on the Year End routine

End of year declarations – when you submit your final payroll details for the tax year, you will be prompted to make a number of declarations similar to those you used to make on the P35 form. The Finish Tax Year wizard guides you through these.

Internet Submission – you must now submit your Year End information to HMRC online. Use this step to submit your final payroll details and declaration information directly to HMRC using Internet Submissions.

- Errors – you must correct any errors that appear before you continue with the submission, such as a missing employee name. To get a paper copy of this information use Print. To stop the submission process, click Cancel and then manually make the correction in your software.
- Warnings – the data preparation process automatically corrects any warnings that appear, such as extra spaces or invalid characters in an employee name. To get a paper copy of this information, use Print. To continue with the submission click Submit. The Submit window appears, displaying the progress of the submission and, when this is complete, the Finished window appears.

Note: Automatic corrections only affect the employee details being submitted to HMRC. The relevant details held in your software do not change.

If the submission was unsuccessful, the report displays error messages advising you what caused the failure.

You can use the e-Submissions log to see a record of your communication history with HMRC.

Sage captures various pieces of information during the submission process. To view this information on the Important Notice window, click the *click here* link.

Sage uses this information for licence validation, troubleshooting issues relating to the Government Gateway and for statistical analysis. None of the personal information held in your software is submitted to Sage. To print this information, use Print.

Beware

Government legislation can change. Make sure you are fully conversant not only with the rates and bandwidths for a payroll year but also any new reporting legislation. Regularly visit the www.gov.uk website for up-to-date information.

Hot tip

RTI makes online payroll reporting to HMRC much simpler than it used to be but make sure you have an active internet connection at all times.

...cont'd

Produce P60s – you must produce a P60 for every employee who is still working for you on 5 April. Employees who left your employment before 5 April must not receive a P60 from you. Check that your P60 forms show the correct tax year.

Instead of paper P60s, you can also email them directly to your employees when producing them during the Payroll Year End process, provided your software is set up to do this.

Take a backup – always take at least one backup before you Complete Year End, though two backups are often recommended.

Complete Year End – here is what this does:

Clearing down the Tax Year deletes records of employees who have left and transfers mileage records from the previous tax year.

- Archives all cumulative year to date values for the current tax year.
- Removes any historical data which has been stored for more than the specified number of years in your software.
- Detects any outstanding balances for Statutory Maternity Pay (SMP), Statutory Paternity Pay (SPP) and Statutory Adoption Pay (SAP). Sage 50 Payroll carries forward the number of weeks already paid, and the amount remaining, then continues to calculate the correct amounts due in the new tax year.
- Carries over cumulative values and outstanding balances for Attachment of Earnings orders. Only the Attachment Value YTD is cleared to zero. This value starts to accumulate from the beginning of the new tax year.
- Carries over the total amount of holiday fund accrued to date.
- Removes any loans that have been completed in the tax year. For example, those with a status of Paid or Written Off. Outstanding balances on all loans remain the same.
- Removes all student loans that were completed in the current tax year.
- If applicable, transfers mileage records from the current tax year, into the new one.

Always make a backup of your data files and label it Year End after clearing YTD Totals.

Distribute P60s – To comply with legislation, you must distribute your employee P60s by 31 May each year.

Preparing for the New Tax Year

For users who may not have access to the internet so that their Payroll program can update automatically or make submissions, here is how to do some of this manually.

Before you start to process your first payroll for the new tax year, you will need to re-enter leave dates for employees who have left the company but were provided with a company car so that liability can be calculated in the next payroll year. Tax codes need updating and any Week 1/Month 1 tax codes need removing.

To re-enter leave dates for leavers with company cars

 Select the leaver and open their Employee Record

 Enter their leaving date in the Employment tab

 Click Save and Close

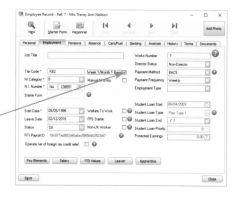

To remove any Week 1/Month 1 codes

1 Select the Employment tab for the relevant Employee Record

2 Click here to deselect this tax code OR use the Global Changes Wizard, Tax Codes option to Set or Clear W1/M1 flags

 Click Save

Updating Tax Codes

To update your tax codes

When updating your tax codes, use the Global Changes Wizard to change information once for a few or all of your records, as shown in the following steps.

To replace one tax code with another

1 From the Tasks menu select Global Changes, Tax Codes, Replace One Tax Code With Another...

2 Enter the existing tax code to change

3 Enter the new tax code to change to

4 Click OK

5 Click Yes to confirm the change

6 Click OK to close the Global Changes Wizard

Hot tip

For help with any queries about Pensions, Loans and all things relating to PAYE you can contact the HMRC Employers Helpline on 0345 200 3200, Monday to Friday, 8:00 am-8:00 pm or 8:00 am-4:00 pm on a Saturday. You will need your employer reference number when you call.

...cont'd

To replace one tax code with another using Prefix

1 From the Tasks menu, select Global Changes, Tax Codes, Apply Tax Code Change Where Code has Prefix...

2 Enter Prefix letter, i.e. K

3 Enter value to change the Tax Code by

4 Click OK

5 Click Yes to confirm

6 Click OK to finish

To replace one tax code with another using Suffix

1 From the Tasks menu select Global Changes, Tax Codes, Apply Tax Code Change Where Code has Suffix...

2 Enter Suffix letter, i.e. L

3 Enter value to change the Tax Code by

4 Click OK

5 Click Yes to confirm

6 Click OK to finish

The Global Changes Wizard will enable you to make changes quickly and easily to Tax Codes, NI Categories, the Payment Rate, Holidays, Payslip Comments, Set or Clear W1/M1 flags and perform a large number of other changes.

Remember to check at the start of the payroll year if there have been any changes to tax codes or the PAYE thresholds.

Updating Tax Bandwidths

With periodic changes in Government legislation, you may need to amend your tax bandwidths in order to calculate your payroll correctly. The steps below show you how to make these changes:

To update your tax bandwidths

1 Click on Legislation... from the Company Tasks list

2 Using the PAYE tab, check the Bandwidths and Rates are correct. Amend any figures which have changed due to new Government legislation. You can request this information by post if you do not have access to the **www.gov.uk** web pages

Hot tip

You can also use the Reports option from the toolbar to check and print out current Government legislation settings.

Legislation Settings - 2016/2017

| PAYE | NI Bands & Rates | SSP | SMP/SAP/SPP/ShPP | Car Details | Student | AEO Rates | Minimum Wage | Childcare | Automatic Enrolment |

Tax bandwidths and rates effective from 06/04/2016   [Add Date] [Edit Date] [Delete Date]

Bandwidth	From	To	Rest of UK Rate (%)	Scottish Rate (%)	Basic Rate Band
32000.00	0.01	32000.00	20.00	20.00	Yes
118000.00	32000.01	150000.00	40.00	40.00	No
excess	150000.01	excess	45.00	45.00	No

Number of Tax Bands 3   Regulatory Deduction Limit % 50
Emergency Tax Code 1100L

Check for online legislation updates ☑
Prompt before performing check ☑

The Legislation Settings shown are for the 2016/2017 Tax Year   [OK] [Cancel]

3 Click on the NI Bands & Rates tab

4 Again, using the latest Government legislation Bandwidths and Rates, carefully check that all the values are correct. Amend any figures which have changed

5 Work through all the remaining tabs, ensuring that all the figures also correspond to the latest Government legislation, amending as necessary

6 After updating all Bandwidth information, click OK to save

Don't forget

Employers are required to deduct student loan repayments from employees who have become liable to repay their loan if it was taken out after August 1998, but no deduction will be made if the salary is below the government set threshold. Check with HMRC for the latest figure.

Advancing Absence and Holiday Year

After completing your Year End procedure you can advance your current holiday and absence year to the new tax year. This option will automatically carry over any unused holiday, but only if your holiday scheme is set up for this.

To advance your absence and holiday year

1 From the Tasks menu select Advance Holiday Year

2 Note the information detailed here before continuing

Advance Holiday Year Wizard

Welcome to the Advance Holiday Year Wizard.

Use this wizard to help you advance your absence and/or holiday year(s) by one year.

Note that holiday accrual by 'Pay Period' is no longer supported in Payroll. Holiday schemes of this type will be changed to 'Daily' method.

Using this wizard at the start of your holiday year will carry over any unused days of holiday, if this is allowed by the relevant holiday scheme.

Cancel   < Back   Next >   Finish

3 Click Next to proceed with the advance, else click Cancel to return to the Payroll Desktop

4 Note the dates listed and remove the tick if you do not wish to advance an item

Advance Holiday Year Wizard

Select the year(s) you want to advance.

Current Absence Year   01/01/2016   ☑ Advance

Current Holiday Year   01/01/2016   ☑ Advance

Click Finish to advance your absence and/or holiday year.

Cancel   < Back   Next >   Finish

5 Click Finish to accept the action

6 Wait whilst the Wizard advances both the absence and holiday years and completes all of the procedures

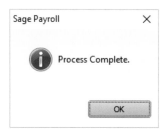

Sage Payroll   ✕

ⓘ Process Complete.

OK

7 Click OK to close and exit the Wizard

16 File Maintenance

Learn the importance of backing up your data files.

Backing Up and Restoring Data

It is very important to keep regular backup copies of your payroll data files. Data can become corrupted, causing a great deal of disruption to the business. For example, loss of payroll information to produce staff wages, time spent re-keying payroll information, fines imposed by HMRC for late returns, etc.

Sage 50 Payroll therefore provides you with the facility to create backups and then restore data files as required.

It is important that you organise and set up a routine for backing up. All backup media must be clearly labelled and kept in a secure place. A minimum of two backup copies need keeping, as media can itself sometimes become faulty. Backup procedures vary. Some businesses use five backup media for Monday to Friday and repeat their usage the following week. The important thing is to remember to back up your data at least once a day when using your Payroll program!

To minimise disruption due to corruption or data entry error, below is a list of times you MUST create backups:

Backup times

AFTER each payroll run but BEFORE updating your records.

AFTER updating your records with each payroll run.

BEFORE making global updates.

BEFORE running your Year End routine.

AFTER running your Year End.

Restoring data

This facility allows you to replace existing data with data from your backup media if, for example, you have made an error whilst processing payroll or the data got corrupted. Whilst Sage Payroll has a Rollback feature, it may be simpler to restore from a backup.

You must be very careful with this option, though. The Restore facility should only be used if there is a problem. You must remember that it restores the data to that at the time of backup, so if any data has been entered since this backup, it will need entering again. Always make sure you are familiar with what you are doing, and repeatedly check that you are restoring from the correct backup file.

It is advisable to keep at least one backup copy of each payroll year, plus you may also find it useful to keep a backup copy for each payroll period in case data needs restoring.

Although mainly reliable, disks and backup media can develop faults through wear and tear, so consider having a minimum of two backup devices to hand.

Backing Up Data

Although Payroll prompts you to take a backup of your data before running certain routines, you should always run this procedure when you have finished with Payroll at the end of the day.

To back up your data

1 From the File menu select Backup

2 Note Backup Wizard details and click Next to continue

3 Select the files you want to include in this backup

4 Click Next to continue

5 Enter a path and filename or Browse to the location

6 Click Next to continue

7 Ensure the backup device, such as a USB drive, is connected to your computer

8 Click Finish to complete the Backup procedure

As Sage prompts you, always make a backup when exiting from the Sage Payroll program.

Data Files are automatically selected for you when creating a backup copy.

Sage default backup filenames refer to the program date, e.g. if payroll date is set to 06/04/2016, filename SAGE0116.001 refers to tax week 1 of year 2016.

Restoring Data

Hopefully you will not need to restore your data but in case your data is corrupted or contains errors, you can use the Restore Wizard BUT remember that restoring will overwrite your current data permanently.

Restoring data will erase all the current data.

1 With your backup device connected, from the File menu, select Restore

2 You can select a backup to restore from in the first window, then click Next

If you need to restore your data you can use the backup filename to identify the tax week.

3 Select the files you need to restore

4 Click Next to continue

5 Type a path and filename or use the Browse button

6 Click Next to continue

Depending on the backup date selected, you may have to re-enter some data.

7 Click Finish to begin the Restore procedure, or click Back to make a change on a previous screen

Restore Wizard

Welcome to the Restore Wizard.

Previous Backups:
You may select a previous backup to be restored from this list.

Date	Time	Company Name	Source Path
22/07/2016	18:11:05	Wizard Train...	C:\ProgramData\Sage\Payroll\COM...
16/11/2016	13:49:24	Wizard Train...	C:\ProgramData\Sage\Payroll\COM...
15/11/2016	15:44:43	Wizard Train...	C:\ProgramData\Sage\Payroll\COM...
14/11/2016	11:26:09	Wizard Train...	C:\ProgramData\Sage\Payroll\COM...
13/11/2016	13:22:14	Wizard Train...	C:\ProgramData\Sage\Payroll\COM...
11/11/2016	15:16:06	Wizard Train...	C:\ProgramData\Sage\Payroll\COM...

Cancel   < Back   Next >   Finish

Restore Wizard

This page enables you to specify which files will be included in the Restore procedure.

Default Files
Data Files
RTI Files
Pension Data Files
Picture Files
Report Files
Template Files
Document Files

Cancel   < Back   Next >   Finish

Restore Wizard

This page lets you choose the file from which to Restore.

You can use the Browse button to browse for a different file, or enter the path and filename manually, if you know it.

Path
G:\Payroll Backup\SagePay.Wizard Training Limited.3516.001   Browse

Cancel   < Back   Next >   Finish

Restore Wizard

The Restore will begin when you click the Finish button.
You may click the Back button if you want to change the details on previous pages.

WARNING!
Restoring from disk will overwrite your current data permanently.

If you are in any doubt choose CANCEL now, then backup your existing data before proceeding.

Cancel   < Back   Next >   Finish

Index

D

E

F

G

H

I

K

L

M

N

O

V

W

Y

31901060151562